WRITING THE X-FILES

Interviews with CHRIS CARTER,
FRANK SPOTNITZ, VINCE GILLIGAN,
JOHN SHIBAN, and HOWARD GORDON

Written By
JASON DAVIS

2016

WRITING THE X-FILES
by Jason Davis

This edition copyright © 2016 by Jason Davis.
All rights reserved.

The moral right of the author has been asserted.

No part of this book may be reproduced or transmitted in any form or by any means electronic or mechanical—including photocopy, recording, Internet posting, electronic bulletin board—or any other information storage and retrieval system, without permission in writing from the Author, except by a reviewer who may quote brief passages in a critical article or review to be printed in a magazine or newspaper, or electronically transmitted on radio, television or in a recognized on-line journal.

The interview recordings from which these newly edited transcripts were derived and these newly edited transcripts are Copyright © 2008 by Jason Davis. All rights reserved.

The X-Files is a trademark of Twentieth Century Fox Film Corporation. All rights reserved.

Portions of the interviews contained herein appeared were previously published as "Why So Mysterious?" and "Tune in for the 'Truth'" in *Creative Screenwriting*, Volume 15, Number 4 (July/August 2008), "Co-Conspirators" in *CS Weekly* (25 July 2008), "No Time Out" in *CS Weekly* (21 November 2008), and "Crystal Method," as by Jason Davis and David Michael Wharton, in *CS Weekly* (6 March 2009). Those articles are Copyright © 2008/2009 by CS Publications.

Cover designed by Jason Davis. Cover photographs copyright © 2016 by Jason Davis. All rights reserved.

Corrected First Edition / March 2016
ISBN: 978-15237-7113-4

For
JEFF & BECKY DAVIS
who got me to
Hollywood (twice),
and for
TERRI NEAL
who kept me there.

Thanks to
Mary Astadourian, Katrina Cabrera-Ortega,
Teo Dell'Amico, Jana Fain, Jeff Goldsmith,
Paul Haas, Elizabeth Harrison, Todd Hoffman,
Laura Jean Leal, Caron McGoldrick,
Lauren McWilliams, Rick Rosen, Gabe Rotter,
Jenny Suen, and Stephen Wolf

Special Thanks to
Chris Carter, Vince Gilligan, Howard Gordon
John Shiban, and Frank Spotnitz

Very Special Thanks to
Richard Allen, Jeffrey Bell,
Jaclyn Easton, Brandon Klassen, Cat Mihos,
Bo Nash, Eric Regalado, Jamie Shahwan,
Den Shewman, and David Michael Wharton

Contents

Foreword:
TWO SUMMERS AT TEN THIRTEEN 9

CHRIS CARTER 15

FRANK SPOTNITZ 37

VINCE GILLIGAN 67

JOHN SHIBAN 103

HOWARD GORDON 115

WHERE ARE THEY NOW? 133

Appendix: WRITING CREDITS 135

Foreword:
TWO SUMMERS AT TEN THIRTEEN

I spent the summer after my junior year of college at *The X-Files*.

My internship at Ten Thirteen Productions was not a rigorously structured affair; I'm not entirely sure anyone remembered that some guy from Texas was *doing* an internship, but I was welcomed by Ten Thirteen Vice President Mary Astadourian when I arrived at Building 41 on the Fox lot, and she put me to work.

Season seven of *The X-Files* was in pre-production, but a lot of my time was spent on *Harsh Realm*, the short-lived series that Chris Carter adapted that season from the comic book by James D. Hudnall and Andrew Paquette. I'd wanted to see how television was written, and thanks to David Amann and Jeff Bell (of *The X-Files*) and Greg Walker and Steven Maeda (of *Harsh Realm*), I got an excellent education in how television writers lived and worked.

X

After grad school, I moved to Los Angeles, and found myself writing for *Creative Screenwriting Magazine*. When it was announced that *The X-Files* would be returning in 2008 with a second feature film, conveniently coinciding with the fifteenth anniversary of the television series, I made my past association known to the editor, and pitched a cover story for the magazine, as well as supporting articles to appear in *CS Weekly*, the online supplement. Thus began my second summer at Ten Thirteen, though this one was entirely telephonic in nature.

To sweeten the deal (for *Creative Screenwriting*, and the readers of this book), I pointed out that I could also ask Howard Gordon about *24* (then at the apex of its popularity) and Vince Gilligan about *Breaking Bad* (which I'd adored from its first shot, but which was not getting any of the attention it would garner later in its run).

I spoke to Chris Carter and Frank Spotnitz a few times during May 2008. *The X-Files: I Want to Believe* was still two months away from being released, and both Chris and Frank were wary of revealing too much of the movie's plot. I focused on *how* they wrote the movie rather than *what* they wrote.

With *The X-Files* having concluded its television run six years before, the retrospective portion of the interviews were a lot of fun. Enough time had passed for the interview subjects to develop a healthy perspective on the show and their time writing it.

Chris and Frank were able to discuss the series much more freely than the upcoming movie, and their interviews provided a lot of leads I'd follow up on in June with the other writers.

John Shiban was just coming off two years on *Supernatural*, a series with more than a little in common with *The X-Files*. After his chat with me, and a stop off at *Legend of the Seeker*, Shiban would join Vince Gilligan on *Breaking Bad* for two years.

Breaking Bad. Those are two words that require a bit of context for readers of this book. Now, you read the words "Breaking Bad," and you think of a television icon. In June 2008, when I spoke with Vince Gilligan, he was hard at work on season two of a little-seen series that had its first year truncated by the Writers Guild of America's 2007–8 strike.

I'd watched the first season of *Breaking Bad* because I saw Vince's name on the press release, but no one else was watching it as far as I could tell. This interview is an interesting snapshot of Vince before Walter White's crimes reached the infamy with which we now regard them.

Howard Gordon—the last of my interviews—had left *The X-Files* in 1996. Because he'd been with Chris at the outset of *The X-Files*, and left when the series was at its apex of popularity, he provided a fascinating look into an earlier era of the pop-culture phenomenon. When we spoke, Howard was midway through his seventh season as showrunner of *24*, so his in-the-thick-of-it thoughts on that landmark television series were an interesting contrast to his insights on *The X-Files*.

If you're wondering about names you *don't* see on the table of contents, know that I did request interviews with a few other folks who, for one reason or another, didn't get back to me during the publication window. In fact, *The X-Files* portion of Howard Gordon's interview wasn't published at the time, because I thought—up to the last minute—that I'd get a few more interviews to publish alongside his. So it goes...

X

As I type these words, *Breaking Bad* has been finished for two and a half years. *24* concluded four years before that (though it returned in 2014 without Howard Gordon at the helm). And *The X-Files* is back on Fox for a six-episode run that compelled me to dust off these interviews.

These are *not* the articles I wrote for *Creative Screenwriting* and *CS Weekly* in 2008; those represented only a fraction of the interview material due to word-count limitations. For this book, I went back to the original audio recordings of the interviews, re-transcribed them, and re-edited them, adding footnotes where I thought they'd be of use.

If you're a fan of *The X-Files*—and if you're not, I think you bought the wrong book—I hope you'll learn something new about the show. I was a serious fan of the series *before* my internship, developed a greater appreciation for everything that went into it *during* my internship, and was ecstatic to conduct these interviews almost a decade *after* the intern became a professional.

Now, I'm excited to revisit the world of Mulder & Scully, Skinner, the Smoking Man, the Lone Gunmen, and Doggett & Reyes—and the writers who created them—with you.

Jason Davis
Los Angeles, CA
28 January 2016

CHRIS CARTER
1 & 22 May 2008

How did you become interested in screenwriting?
Really from my wife. I was working as a journalist when I met her. She was a screenwriter[1], working for a long time in the industry, and convinced me to write a screenplay of a story that I held near and dear.

Did that screenplay land you an agent?
It was read by an agent who liked it very much, would not represent me, but sent the script out. The script got very good notices; I did meetings around town. I was convinced or encouraged to write another script,

---

[1] Dori Carter (*née* Pierson), wrote the tv movies *The Imposter* (1984, co-written with Eric Hendershot and Marc Rubel), *Obsessed with a Married Woman* (1985, screenplay co-written with Carol Sobieski from a story by Beverly J. Camhe and Arlene Sidaris), *Prince of Bel Air* (1986, co-written with Marc Rubel), and the feature film *Big Business* (1988, co-written with Marc Rubel). As Dori Carter, she's published the novel BEAUTIFUL WASPS HAVING SEX (2000) and the short story collection WE ARE RICH (2007).

which I did, which was read by [Walt Disney Company Chairman] Jeff Katzenberg. The next thing I knew I was in the movie business.

How did you move from movies into television?
I was working at Walt Disney, the "New Disney," at the time, [CEO Michael] Eisner and Katzenberg [were there]. I was sitting in my office and all these producers kept coming by and asking if I was interested in doing Disney Sunday movies. Because I was excited and hungry, I said yes to all of them.[2]

Did that work lead to your eventual development deal with Fox?
Yes…that's the long way around. I did some television pilots[3] and Disney Sunday movies. I quickly realized being there—I think maybe I was there for just under two years—that if I really wanted to make myself happy, I would need to learn how to produce and so I did that. I took a job as a producer on a tv series[4] and started learning the ropes.

---

[2] Carter wrote *The B.R.A.T. Patrol* (1986, co-written with Michael Patrick Goodman) and *Meet the Munceys* (1988) for *Walt Disney's Wonderful World of Color*.

[3] Among the pilots Carter wrote and produced were *Cameo By Night* (1987), concerning a police secretary (Sela Ward) who goes undercover as a rock'n'roll fan to hunt a serial killer preying upon concert goers; and *Brand New Life*, which debuted with a two-hour movie as part of a rotating wheel of Disney programs, in 1989 and ran for five further episodes (1989–90). It featured Barbara Eden and Don Murray playing the parents of a newly fused family, á là *The Brady Bunch*. In THE TRUTH IS OUT THERE: THE OFFICIAL GUIDE TO THE X-FILES (Harper Prism, 1995), author Brian Lowry notes at least two further pilots Carter wrote prior to *The X-Files*: the science-fiction series *Copter Cop* and the surfing-themed *Cool Culture*.

[4] Carter's first producing job was on *Rags to Riches* (1987–8), created by Bernie Kukoff.

That led to a job at NBC Productions, working under Brandon Tartikoff[5] developing television pilots. I developed several things there, including something that was short lived on the Disney Sunday Movie wheel, coincidentally, because I had just worked for Disney.

After that, Peter Roth—who had seen my work when he was [president] at [Stephen J. Cannell Productions]—had called me in a number of times to see if I wanted to run television shows for Stephen Cannell.[6] I had always declined, but when he took over as the head of Twentieth Television, he brought me over to develop television pilots for 20th Century Fox exclusively.

---

[5] Brandon Tartikoff (1949–97) was the president of NBC from 1980 to 1991, presiding over the network's rise to the pinnacle of US television and inventing the "Must-See-TV" Thursday night lineup that remained a ratings powerhouse even after his death. Among the iconic television series he championed during his tenure at NBC were: *Hill Street Blues*, *L.A. Law*, *Law & Order*, *ALF*, *Family Ties*, *The Cosby Show*, *Cheers*, *Seinfeld*, *The Golden Girls*, *Wings*, *Miami Vice*, *Punky Brewster*, *Knight Rider*, *The A-Team*, *Saved By the Bell*, *St. Elsewhere*, and *Night Court*. After NBC, Tartikoff briefly served as the Chairman of Paramount Pictures, where he helped develop *Star Trek: Deep Space Nine*. *Beggars and Choosers*, Showtime's satire of the television business was co-created by Tartikoff and Peter Lefcourt; it was produced and broadcast after the former's death.

[6] After launching his career as a freelance writer on series like *Ironside* and *Columbo*, Stephen J. Cannell (1941–2010) achieved fame as the co-creator and producer of *The Rockford Files* before launching his own production company in 1979. Stephen J. Cannell Productions—with its iconic logo of Cannell ripping a page of script from his typewriter—was a major provider of one-hour dramatic series for US television, producing—among others—*The Greatest American Hero*, *The A-Team*, *Hardcastle and McCormick*, *Wiseguy*, *21 Jump Street*, *Silk Stalkings*, and *The Commish*. Cannell pioneered the production of US television in Canada, basing most of his late 1980s productions in Vancouver. In 1995, he sold off his production company and devoted the last fifteen years of his life to writing novels.

You've said that *Kolchak: The Night Stalker*[7] was a big influence on *The X-Files*. What about that series inspired you?
It was scary and it was good. It had left a big impression on me as a kid. I think I actually watched those shows—for some reason, I watched them alone—and I remember just being completely petrified watching them.

I couldn't believe no one had done something as scary as that on television [since then], and so there was an opportunity.

Were there any other notable influences on *The X-Files* pilot?
You can see *The Silence of the Lambs*—which had just come out, and which I liked very much—was a big influence on it. Scully's character is not dissimilar from Clarice Starling, so that was a big influence.[8]

---

[7] *The Night Stalker*, adapted by Richard Matheson from Jeff Rice's then-unpublished novel, became ABC's highest-rated movie-of-the-week in 1972, spurring a 1973 sequel movie, *The Night Strangler*, as well as a short-lived television series, *Kolchak: The Night Stalker* (1974–5). In 2005, *X-Files* veteran Frank Spotnitz revived the concept as *Night Stalker*. Only six of the ten produced episodes were broadcast by ABC, but the series reunited *X-Files* writers Darin Morgan, Thomas Schnauz, and Vince Gilligan.

Carter's debt to the series was acknowledged onscreen in "Little Green Men," where Agent Mulder's congressional patron was named Senator Richard Matheson. Darin Morgan's unproduced script for ABC's 2005 *Night Stalker* revival was re-written as "Mulder and Scully Meet the Were-Monster" for *The X-Files* revival in 2016.

[8] The 1992 Academy Award®-winning Best Picture *The Silence of the Lambs* was based on novelist Thomas Harris's second book to explore the world of profiling serial killers, a subject that formed the basis for Chris Carter's next television series, *Millennium* (1996–9).

The idea of science versus faith—or the paranormal or the supernatural—was interesting to me, generally. When I read that there were scientific studies being done about aliens and the existence of extraterrestrials, I thought it was really an interesting opportunity to use that as a central theme for a television show.

What did you look for in hiring writers for *The X-Files*?
It's sort of a stab in the dark, because when a show's coming online, what you do is you try and find the best writers possible, and hope they develop a connection to the material. I was most fortunate in hiring just the right people at just the right time. I hired a fantastic team who wrote some of the best episodes during the first season: Glen Morgan and James Wong.[9] I also hired two very, very talented writers: Howard Gordon and Alex Gansa.[10] That was really the core writing unit for the first season.

---

[9] Glen Morgan and James Wong came to *The X-Files* after working at Stephen J. Cannell Productions on *21 Jump Street*, *Wiseguy*, and *The Commish*. They worked at Ten Thirteen Productions until midway through season two of *The X-Files*, returning briefly in season four, and then served as showrunners for Chris Carter's *Millennium* during its second season. After leaving Ten Thirteen Productions and 20th Century Fox, Morgan and Wong launched the *Final Destination* film franchise before dissolving their partnership circa 2005. In 2015, Morgan and Wong returned to Ten Thirteen Productions to separately write, produce, and direct one episode each of the resurrected *X-Files*.

[10] Howard Gordon and Alex Gansa came to *The X-Files* after working at Witt/Thomas Productions on *Beauty and the Beast* and Lorimar Television's *Sisters*. After their first season on *The X-Files*, Gordon and Gansa's writing partnership dissolved, and Gansa departed the series. Gordon remained through season four, departing to work on *Buffy the Vampire Slayer* in 1996. The one-time partners were eventually reunited on Fox's *24*, and together they developed *Homeland* for Showtime.

After that first season, writers like Frank Spotnitz and John Shiban didn't have television credits before *The X-Files*. Were you looking for writers new to the medium?
It's great to find a new writer because you get the tremendous amount of enthusiasm. People who have never seen their work put up on screen before are hungry, so that's always a nice thing to do. Having people who are hungry always helps.

Frank mentioned that he came to the show not knowing what was possible, and images like the submarine conning tower breaking through the ice in "End Game" were a result of that naïveté. Does not knowing what's impossible in television allow you to do things you wouldn't otherwise do?
I think you can say that all of us were so enthusiastic and ultimately naïve about what could or couldn't be done in television that we tried to do everything. Somehow, we pulled most things off.

That conning tower, and the ice with a refrigerated stage, tons of snow trucked in…if you really had your veteran producer's cap on, you probably wouldn't try something like that because you know not only is it costly, but it's just so hard. There was nothing we thought was too hard in the beginning, and that really helped us out.

Did the method you used to break stories in the first season change by the end of the series's nine-year run?
Essentially, it was the same from beginning to end. Morgan and Wong had brought with them a very streamlined but rigorous approach to plotting. They'd sit in front of a bulletin board with 3x5 cards, and

you'd plot on those cards. By the end, you'd have a series of tiles. You can look at your board and it not only has a narrative—you can see the narrative—but you can sort of see the visual rise and fall of the plot points.

It was very good because no one was sitting with an outline in front of them, [with] everyone bringing to it their own impressions. Everyone was able sit in the room, look at a board, and see the flow of the story.

Did the network or the studio have a problem with the ambiguity remaining at the end of so many of *The X-Files* episodes?
Yes. In the beginning, they wanted everything wrapped up; they wanted the unexplained explained, and it took a little bit of convincing for them to understand that the show was better if everything was left open.

How did Gillian Anderson's second-season pregnancy factor into the development of the show's mythology?
It was a problem to be solved, and there are different ways we [considered] solving it.

Ultimately, it was landed on—and it was a group thing—that we shoot around her pregnancy, and have her taken away.[11] There was talk about having her impregnated, that she would have an alien baby. It was a good choice not to do that.

---

[11] Anderson's Dana Scully was written out in "Ascension," the sixth episode of season two, was absent for "3," the seventh episode, and returned from her maternity leave in episode eight, "One Breath."

The Cigarette Smoking Man (William B. Davis) made his first appearance in the pilot, but didn't speak; he's just there, smoking. What compelled you to make him the antagonist for much of the series?

I thought he was an interesting character who was even more villainous by his silence—he was completely cold and calculating—this looming government presence who was only looking out for his own interests.

When you featured the Smoking Man in the pilot, did you imagine bigger things for him later on in the series?

In the beginning, you're playing for one script at a time, and trying to take off and catch fire, as it were.

When you are imagining that character, and how he's going to fit into the overall series… People claim that they're imagining ten episodes ahead. I think that they're fudging, because you don't imagine ten episodes ahead; you're working so hard just to stay on the air, you don't have that luxury.

I always had a sense of where I was going. I had a goal, but I didn't know how I was going to get there. I think that's a function of what the actors bring to the characters, what their strengths are, how they start to develop. You must do things organically; you can't just set a course and sail it. The winds change, the weather changes—actors get pregnant, for example—and you have to use that.

Your writing staff also plays a huge part. Everyone brings something. The interesting thing about a television series is that the whole staff brings something to the table. The contributions of Glen Morgan, James Wong, Howard Gordon, and Alex Gansa were to quality, taste, and process. They played a huge part in *The X-Files*'s success.

How did directing "Duane Barry" change you as a writer?
You realize very quickly that you think you have imagined it all as a writer, that you have a perfect understanding of the story and that everyone else need only to read the script well in order to have that perfect understanding too. When you have to actually put the characters in a scene in time and space and move them around, there are so many things that you realize as a writer you haven't thought about.

It made me appreciate more that what we do is a visual medium. As a storyteller, you must be cognizant at all times of how the writer's intention can be fulfilled only by the interesting and complex reality that you create as a director.

How did your writing partnership with Frank Spotnitz on the mythology episodes develop?
It developed because I had writers leaving the show [at the end of the second season].[12] I called Frank in, because I knew he was a smart person. The first thing he worked on was a mythology episode ["End Game"]. It happened—almost coincidentally—that he and I would

---

[12] Morgan and Wong departed *The X-Files* midway through season two to produce the pilot of *Space: Above and Beyond* (1995–6), which ran for one season on Fox alongside the third season of *The X-Files*. After Fox cancelled *Space* at the end of its freshman year, Morgan and Wong returned to *The X-Files* in season four, bolstering the writing staff while Carter launched the first season of *Millennium* (1996–9).

start to develop that mythology arc as a series of two-parters that would go the length and span of the show. It developed by chance.

What was your process when writing mythology episodes together?
We really worked carefully in the plotting process, and then I would take the first swipe at the script. [That was] generally the way it worked.

As a writer, what was the most difficult episode for you to write and why?
I had trouble with an episode called "Fire." It was difficult because we were in full-swing production—I think it was episode seven or eight [of the first season]—and once you get that far in, you have lots of things happening. You're running full-tilt. With a show in its infancy, there are lots of unforeseen problems.

One of the unforeseen problems for me was that the hills of Malibu were on fire and I lived close by. I could actually walk down my street and see the fires heading toward me as I was writing an episode called "Fire." It made for a very nail-biting writing experience.

Were there any stories that just never worked out, that you wanted to tell but couldn't break?
Yes. There was a story we worked very hard on. The writers worked very hard with a freelance writer. We could never crack the story about life after death.[13]

---

[13] See the Frank Spotnitz interview for more on this unproduced story.

How did you learn to run a writers' room?
I'd actually done some work in writers' rooms before. I'd worked on several different series, including one short-lived series that I created for Brandon Tartikoff. I had done it before, but I'd never done it quite in this fashion.

I was blessed with having experienced writers—Glen Morgan and James Wong; Howard Gordon and Alex Gansa—who had actually done it before. Basically, it was people sitting in a room spitballing, really. Just throwing ideas out, coming in with an idea and everyone pitching in early on.

There is no way a writers' room should be run. Everyone should be free to throw out ideas and not feel ashamed of throwing out bad ideas, because sometimes what you think is a bad idea might be a good idea, or a riff on it. I don't think there's any way to run a writers' room. Every combination of writers and writers' room runs differently.

Did you have a bible for the series?
No. No bible for the series. I think that can be a trap.

Do you feel it limits the possibilities for the show?
I think that if you start trying to hit marks it takes away the adventure of discovery.

The person who—starting after season two—really began running the writers' room, was Howard Gordon. When Howard left after season four, Frank really took on that role. He was aided by two other people—who did a very good job—Vince Gilligan and John Shiban. I think Vince Gilligan did some of the best work ever on *The X-Files*.

Speaking of John, Frank, and Vince, do you recall anything particular about the writing of "Memento Mori?"
Yes, I do. You may have been told this story, but those guys wrote a script, which was in prep as we went to Christmas vacation. I took it with me to Hawai'i and went through it very carefully. I did that before Frank got to Hawai'i. [Then] Frank and I worked on boarding the first *X-Files* movie. It was not my wife's idea of a vacation.

"Memento Mori" was written as you were boarding the movie?
Yes, it was. That was an Emmy-nominated script.[14] It blew my mind.

Frank said the board for that story was concocted at the last minute when another script fell out.
The board was, and then the script was done quickly. Then I took that script with me. I went through it on my own over that Christmas vacation.[15]

---

[14] "Momento Mori" was nominated for the 1997 Primetime Emmy Award for Outstanding Writing for a Drama Series. The script lost to the *NYPD Blue* episode "Where's Swaldo?" written by Stephen Gaghan, David Milch, and Michael R. Perry. Perry subsequently joined the writing staff of Chris Carter's *Millennium*.

Carter was also nominated in the same category for "Duane Barry" (in 1995) and "The Post-Modern Prometheus" in 1999.

[15] For more on the writing of "Momento Mori," see the Frank Spotnitz interview.

I once had something so strange happen. My wife and I—it may have been a year or two later—we went for Christmas vacation to Costa Rica. A teenage girl was there with her family. Someone told her who I was, and she came up to me and recited—from memory—the opening Scully monologue from ["Momento Mori"].

Was it strange to encounter your words in a foreign country?
It was weird for a kid to come up to you, and have something that you worked on [memorized]. It's very strange when things like that happen.

Frank said "Milagro" mirrored the experience of writing *The X-Files*. Did you find that to be the case?
Yes, I did. That was an interesting experience for me also because Frank and John had come up with an idea, and they basically handed me the idea and I did the script. Usually, it doesn't work that way.

How did writing the first feature—*The X-Files: Fight the Future*—in 1998 change your perspective as a writer?
Hard to say. It was a trick, trying to do a television show and a movie of the television show at the same time. They needed to relate to one another, yet the movie was so much bigger than the television show that it had the effect of creating a before-the-movie era of *The X-Files* and an after-the-movie era.

It also coincided with our move to Los Angeles.[16] I'd have to say the whole thing was rather audacious on our part.

When I look back on it now, I think it was a good idea, but it's something that a regular series should think twice about, because it is a huge undertaking.

Did you ever feel that the mythology was getting away from you? Was the partial dismantling of the mythology in the first movie your effort to reign it in after four years?
No. I feel that we always had a hold of it, and that it was always interesting to us, and hopefully interesting to the audience.

What happens is that you never know how long a tv series is going to run. When you set out, you hope to go five years. Then, all of a sudden, when you're going six and seven and eight and nine and ten, you've got to ask yourself how far and fast should I go with anything because you never know when you're going to have to resolve [it]. In pacing and in direction and in evolution, we did nine seasons of the show and we did 202 episodes well.

I was very surprised when *The Sopranos* ended, and had done [eighty-

---

[16] *The X-Files: Fight the Future* was filmed in Los Angeles in the summer of 1997, between the Vancouver-based seasons four and five of the series. The feature film's lengthy post-production period coincided with the broadcast of season five (1997–8), and the movie was released on 19 June 1998, a month after season five concluded. When the television series resumed for its sixth season on 8 November 1998, production had relocated to Los Angeles.

six] episodes. These are two different approaches to series television.

Do you think a definite end point—as the writers of *Lost* secured—would have been a benefit to *The X-Files*?
It could have been. It would have eliminated a lot of really good work if we would have done that. There was a lot of good work done in seasons six through nine, so while that's a luxury, it's a luxury we didn't have. Fox wasn't going to take the show off; whether I stayed with it or not, they were determined to go on. I decided to stay with it the entire time because I felt that it would benefit the show.

When you introduced Special Agents John Doggett (Robert Patrick) and Monica Reyes (Annabeth Gish) in season eight, how did you go about changing the leads of your show without alienating the audience in the process?
No one teaches you this stuff. You try to figure out what is most interesting to you, and you try to figure out characters who are different than the characters that you have on the show.

When adding a new character, there's always a risk associated, but there's always a reward associated as well, because you are complicating the existing relationships. You're adding a complexity and a dynamic to the show by the addition of anything. I think if you're able to take any problem and turn it into a virtue, then you've done your job as a producer and a writer.

Do you have anything you'd like to share about "Improbable?"
It was an episode you could only do after having developed a hit show. It's an improbable episode in itself, and it had to do with my reading on theoretical physics and the laws of probability. Also, it was a chance for me to do something musically strange. I love that episode.

I loved working with Burt Reynolds and it's also a very strange thing—as a writer and as a director and as a producer—to work with somebody who had such impact on you in your youth: Burt Reynolds in *The Longest Yard* and *Sharky's Machine* and *Deliverance*. To work with someone like that was a thrill.

What episode of *The X-Files* are you proudest of?
It's always hard to say. There were a couple of episodes that I wrote and directed which were near and dear to my heart. One is a black-and-white [episode] called "The Post-Modern Prometheus," and another one I wrote and directed called "Triangle." I like those episodes because they did things that only a successful tv series can do: they took chances.[17]

Beyond that, there were so many episodes I really loved of *The X-Files*, and they weren't necessarily my own.

Which of the episodes you didn't write come to mind?
"Bad Blood" [by Vince Gilligan] was an excellent episode. "Beyond the

---

[17] Carter was nominated for Outstanding Writing and Outstanding Directing for a Drama Series at the 1999 Primetime Emmy Awards for his work on "The Post-Modern Prometheus."

Sea" [by Glen Morgan and James Wong]—terrific. "Clyde Bruckman's Final Repose"[18] and "Jose Chung's FROM OUTER SPACE" [both by Darin Morgan]. I think those…

"Home" [by Morgan and Wong], of course.

Did the controversial nature of "Home" appeal to you?[19]
Yeah, and I just thought it was well done.

When you look at tv in 2008, what influence do you detect from *The X-Files*?
I don't know. I think you just take any successful tv show and it really opens doors for another approach.

This idea that we were successful with doing a mythology seems to have been something that gave people confidence to do [shows] like *24*; you could do a series of episodes that were interrelated and required a knowledge of the tv series. I always say those are the hardest kinds of concepts, because if people don't come in the beginning, they're not going to come later.

I think our ambition was to do something special each week, and if we

---

[18] "Clyde Bruckman's Final Repose" won two of *The X-Files*'s sixteen Primetime Emmy Awards: Outstanding Writing for a Drama Series for Darin Morgan, and Outstanding Guest Actor in a Drama Series for Peter Boyle as Clyde Bruckman.

[19] "Home" was originally broadcast by Fox on 11 October 1996. It was rated TV-MA, and featured viewer discretion warning. Fox declined to ever repeat the episode, and it was not screened again in the US until FX syndicated the series.

succeeded in doing that, I think it gave other people the opportunities to try similar things.

Why do you think it is the right time for a second *X-Files* film?
We've been away from Mulder (David Duchovny) and Scully (Gillian Anderson) for just long enough that there's an appetite for them. It would have seemed like an extension of the tv show, I think, if the movie would have come any sooner. [Six years] allowed us to step back and take a look at those characters and at the concept and decide how to approach it now at a distance.

How has your writing changed since the series ended?
The sheer volume of writing has hopefully honed my abilities. I think I know what works and what doesn't, what plays and what doesn't, but that's a constant struggle. You really don't know, but you have instincts that are developed and honed.

In the end, everything you write plays or doesn't based on the actors. You can write the best script in the world, but if you don't have a terrific cast to perform, you sink. There's no such thing as a bullet-proof script.

Was it easier not having to fit *I Want to Believe*'s story into a gap in the tv show's continuity?
Yes. That was a really nice thing, not having those episodes stretching out over the horizon that you had to think about while you are doing a movie, which takes a pinpoint focus.

How long did it take to write the screenplay for *I Want to Believe*?
From April to August [2007].

Is *I Want to Believe* a mythology-related story, or more of a monster-of-the-week standalone?
It's a stand-alone episode, and can be called a monster-of-the-week episode. I think, like some of the best *X-Files*, it takes place within the realm of extreme possibility.

How does writing Mulder and Scully in a post-9/11 world differ from before?
I think there are different eras of post-9/11. There was the "near-era," a very fearful time when we put all our faith in our government to protect us.

As time has gone on, I think we are losing faith in our government and in our leaders because we feel that we are not necessarily being told the whole picture. That has led to certain transgressions, which I think are scary now in a way that they were scary before 9/11—in a post-Watergate era—so I think we've come full circle, even though I still think that expression "full-circle" is inapplicable only because we are now different because of that 9/11 experience.

What was the toughest challenge in writing *I Want to Believe*?
Keeping it a secret. Imagining the characters six years down the road and being honest about it.

Will *I Want to Believe* play upon the Mulder and Scully romantic relationship that was always hinted at in the series but never really addressed directly beyond the existence of their baby?
Yes. We deal with that relationship and its…ramifications.

Did you have any notes from Fox on the screenplay for *I Want to Believe*?
We had notes, and I have to say they helped make the script better.

Can you specify in which way the notes helped?
[The studio] had a very good take on the story. One of the notes led to one of the few scenes that was deleted from the movie, but I have to say, overall, their notes were very astute in terms of character, plot, and pace.

Did you have notes from Duchovny and/or Anderson?
Yes. Both David and Gillian had very good notes. In fact, David had a note that I incorporated hours before the writers' strike.[20]

So there was some last-minute tweaking before the strike began?
Yes. [David and Gillian] are very smart about their characters and always have been.

That also is a benefit that you have when you have intelligent input, when you have people who have a very smart take on their character. It always adds to the script.

---

[20] The Writers Guild of America went on strike on 5 November 2007. Due to the WGA's rules, Carter and Spotnitz were not allowed to alter the movie's script while the strike was in force.

As the director, were you able to fine tune your story without altering the script?

We had worked very hard, knowing the writers' strike was coming. We didn't know exactly when it was coming—it came earlier than when we imagined—but we'd worked very hard to get the script exactly where we wanted it before that time. We were working at a breakneck pace because Fox had told us we had to.

What, if anything, did you learn from doing *Fight the Future* that you employed on *I Want to Believe* that changed the way you approached this movie from the way you did the last one?

I don't know if that's an applicable question because we had about half the budget on this movie. The lessons I learned were really what I took from the television series about showing less, implying more, keeping things in the shadows. Things are often scarier that you don't see rather than what you do see, so it was really lessons I learned from the television series.

How difficult has it been to keep spoilers about *I Want to Believe* off the internet?

It's extremely difficult, and we've had a lot of practice at it. To date, we have kept the story a secret. I don't know if we'll actually be able to do that until opening day, but we took measures to prevent people from finding out.

Can you describe these measures?

Propaganda is an effective tool in the fight against spoilers.

Have you seeded the internet with misinformation?
[Misinformation] is always a weapon in your arsenal.

If you could give a new writer one piece of advice, what would it be?
Keep your mind open. Rewrite; it always can be made better. Never forsake the note-giving process or undervalue it.

What time of day do you usually write?
I write any time of day. Now, I have to say, I try not to write after dinner.

Do you ever suffer from writer's block?
When you grow up writing television, you're not allowed to have writer's block.

Provided *I Want to Believe* does well at the box office, do you see it as the first in a long line of post-series movies?
No. I don't see it as the first of a long line. I see it as—if we're successful—possibly as an opportunity to do another *X-Files* movie, but only time and box office receipts will tell.

You don't see *The X-Files* as an ongoing film franchise like *Star Trek*?
I only want to do it as long as David and Gillian want to do it. Who knows how long that will be?

FRANK SPOTNITZ
1 & 19 May 2008

How did you become interested in screenwriting?
I have a long answer, because it's my second career.

I started out as a reporter. I wrote for the wire services and for magazines and became disenchanted with being a reporter. At first I tried my hand at being a novelist and I really was not cut out for that. Then I realized that movies and television are what I really grew up with—even more than literature—and so I moved back to Los Angeles after having been a reporter for seven years. I was living in Paris at that point.

I moved to Los Angeles, went to the American Film Institute, and got my MFA in screenwriting. *The X-Files* was my first job out of film school.

How did you land *The X-Files* job?

By dumb luck. When I moved back to Los Angeles, I got into a book group through some friends. It was like eight or ten people in this book group, and among those people was Chris Carter. At the time, he was writing tv movies for Disney and we were in this book group together for a couple of years. The book group ended, and I didn't really see him or speak to him.

Then *The X-Files* came onto tv and I started watching it 'cause I knew who Chris was and I thought it was great. I never thought about calling him or trying to write for the show—it just never crossed my mind. I thought I was going to write movies anyway; I didn't think I was going to write for television at all.

Toward the end of the first season, a friend of mine called me who was an aspiring television writer. He said, "You know this guy Chris Carter, don't you?" I said, "Yeah," and he said, "Will you call him for me and see if he'll let me come and pitch some ideas?" I was pretty uncomfortable, because I didn't know him *that* well, but I figured why not? I'll do it.

I called him and he said, "No, I won't hear your friend's ideas, but I'll hear yours if you have any." I didn't have any but I thought well, I haven't sold any of my screenplays yet…I'm still supporting myself by writing for magazines…what's the harm…I might as well give it a shot.

I took a few weeks and I thought up three ideas. I called him up and scheduled a meeting for me to come in and pitch the ideas. He promptly shot them all down, all three, didn't buy any of them. I thought, well, that was the end of that; that was pretty much a waste of time.

Only a few weeks later, he called me—it was a Thursday, I remember—and he said, "I didn't buy any of your ideas, but they were all good, and here's what was good about each one of them. So, while I didn't buy any of your ideas, I'm losing some writers and I do have an opening for a staff writer if you'd like to come on board full-time." That was a Thursday, and I started on Monday, and that was it.

I started as a staff writer knowing absolutely nothing about television production. Within three years, I was an executive producer at the show.

How did you end up with a mythology episode ["End Game"] for your first script?
It kind of worked out that way. It's all just luck, really.

After I'd been hired, we went to lunch and [Chris] was asking me what ideas I had. One of my first ideas was: it's been so long since Mulder has seen his sister and—she was a little girl when he saw her last—if an adult woman came to him, looked even remotely like his sister and claimed to be her, how would he know it wasn't? [Chris] loved that idea, and he asked me to marry it to an idea that David Duchovny had about an alien bounty hunter.

That became the first episode. It was a two-part episode, and I worked on both parts, but I ended up being credited solely for the second part, which was called "End Game."

Was there a value in not having prior television experience before coming to *The X-Files*?

From my point of view, there was, because I had no idea what the limitations of television were. That was a theme that was pretty consistent my first two or three years on the show; I was writing things that were unproducable. That started with my first episode.

["End Game"] was just jam-packed with all kinds of action. We had to take out an enormous amount [of material] just to make it filmable. Even then, we kept in this huge submarine conning tower that we built, that had to break through the ice. It was an enormous thing to do for television, to build the conning tower and freeze a sound stage and cart in thousands of tons of snow, but we did that.

The next episode I wrote ["Our Town"] was more contained. It was a stand-alone, scary episode.

The next mythology thing I did ["Nisei" and "731"] had moving trains, which were unheard of. Nobody's going to do that on television. What was amazing was that—every time out—we ended up finding a way to do it.

It became a part of the show that these mythology episodes—that I ended up becoming identified with—invariably were made for sweeps. Because they were made for sweeps, the studio was able to open their purse a little more and give us greater resources to produce them. It kept feeding the growth and the ambition of the show. It didn't hurt that the ratings of the show kept growing as well; the first five years [of] *The X-Files* had a bigger audience every year.

How did the mythology-writing partnership with Chris evolve?
It was sort of natural. After that first two-parter—"Colony" and "End Game"—proved to be so successful, it was just natural that I would end up having something to do with all of the mythology episodes after that. That was a really important episode in the mythology of the series. It was something I had a feel for and was interested in.

Unfortunately, as far as I'm concerned, selfishly, my name ended up being on many of the mythology episodes, and people think that's all I had to do with the show—"Oh, he did all the mythology." No, that's not true; I was really involved in all the episodes, all the scary, stand-alone episodes. With a few exceptions, I was just as deeply involved with them as the mythology, but that's the perception of me—by those who pay attention to who wrote what—that [the mythology] was my only interest.

You were also one-third of the "John Gilnitz" triumvirate.
That was a lot of fun.

How did writing with John Shiban and Vince Gilligan differ from writing with Chris?
Well, Chris was sort of a towering figure. He was very demanding and competitive and he had very specific ideas about what the show was.

Everyone who came to work for the show—everyone who succeeded—did so by understanding Chris's vision and contributing to it; they didn't stray from it. They got it, because it was very clear and then they added to it. Once you got what it was he wanted, you could then bring to it things he never would have thought of.

John and Vince and I were all in the same boat, in a way, in that we were the hired help, so it wasn't like working with the head of the company; it was like working with your colleagues. It was always fun when the three of us would write something.

We started this "John Gilnitz" thing because the first episode we did together ["Leonard Betts"]—where the three of us were sort of called in to rewrite—that was our inside joke, to put a character named John Gilnitz in there. Then we just ended up doing it more and more, because we just had so much fun doing it together.

I particularly remember two episodes—"Leonard Betts," which was shown after the Super Bowl in season four, and the two-part episode called "Dreamland" we did in season six—where we ended up laughing so much in the process of writing it that it was just a joy.

I can't say that there were an awful lot of things [that] were a joy during *The X-Files*, because it was such hard work. It was very demanding, and we pushed ourselves very, very hard, so whenever you could get some laughs in, it was really welcome.

When you were collaborating on a script, did you divide it up by acts, scenes, or just pass drafts from writer to writer for revision?
We've done it all different ways. We would invariably do the outline together, and we outlined by working on a bulletin board with those index cards. Then, when it came time to write the script, sometimes we would just split it up and each do an act; that's usually when we were very short on time. When that happened, somebody has to go back and rewrite; it was always Chris in the first several seasons. With the later seasons, it was sort of Chris and Vince who became the primary re-writers of scripts.

Other times, we wrote them together, like "Leonard Betts." I remember John, Vince, and I writing together. On "Dreamland," I remember going to Vince's house and laughing a lot because it's an outright comedy, and we just wrote it together, throwing out lines. I'd say it's probably a lot slower that way, but it was fun.

How did you change as a writer after directing "Alone?"
The thing that made the biggest impact on me as a writer was not directing, really, it was editing. That was one of the great things that Chris did: he welcomed—encouraged, even—writers to go to the editing room. You learn an enormous amount about filmmaking by editing, because you see how film cuts together, what pieces of film you need to tell a story. You realize where a script goes wrong when you're editing something together. You realize when you don't need that part of a scene, or the scene became about something else here, so you want to cut that out.

I did an awful lot of editing on the show. From my first week, I was invited into the editing room. There was an episode ["Excelsis Dei"] that was in trouble, and even though I'd never edited before, they asked me to go in and help.

By the time I got around to directing—which was very late in the run of the series—I had a pretty solid understanding of how things cut together. The thing I didn't appreciate was how bulky and unwieldy the camera is. That was a surprise to me as a director, how hard it was to move the camera. I had some very elaborate moves I wanted to make—which I still did make—but it was harder than I anticipated.

My appreciation for actors—which was already pretty great—only increased. I think that's probably the main thing I got out of directing versus editing, a sensitivity to how careful you have to be to make sure your scenes have a logic that tracks from moment to moment because the actor has to make that work. If it doesn't work on the page, it's going to be very difficult for the actor to make it work on the screen. That was the biggest thing that directing helped me to understand.

At what point did you realize that you were riding a massive pop-culture phenomenon?
There was a sense that it was a growing hit, and I could sense it because when I first started working for the show, not that many people I knew had heard of it. By season three, many people had heard of it, and by season four, it was a big fat hit. It never really did feel that real to us, even when we were going to fan conventions. So much of your experience is being in your office, or the offices of your colleagues, working

and editing. You're really cloistered, and not in touch with the fans and the reality of how many people you're reaching.

It's only now—six years after the show has ended—that we're doing this movie, and I'm seeing this phenomenal response from the fans who are still out there. You realize this really did reach a lot of people, and they still remember it and they still care about it. I don't think I've really appreciated it until now.

What episodes are you proudest of, and why?
I have many episodes that I'm proud of and that I admire. I think—because I really love the show as a fan as much as a writer—so many of the ones that are my favorite episodes are ones that I had very little to do with—episodes that were written before I came on to the show—like the pilot, "The Host," "Beyond the Sea," "Ice," or episodes that were done by writers who really were entities unto themselves like Darin Morgan, who wrote "Humbug" and "Clyde Bruckman's Final Repose," for which he won an Emmy.

The episode that I think is the most successful—of all the mythology episodes—was called "Momento Mori," which I wrote with John, Vince, and Chris. We got nominated for an Emmy for that as well, in season four. That's the one where Scully finds out she has cancer.

I love an episode we did in season six called "Milagro." It's really an autobiographical episode about a writer who's obsessed with Scully, and it really spoke to what it was like to be a writer on *The X-Files*. You spend so much of your life thinking about fictitious characters that they really became kind of real to you. That's probably the two that had my name on [them] that I feel the fondest toward.

Why is "Milagro" special to you?
It's interesting to me, the whole process of writing. It's a fantastic way to spend your life, because no one ever masters writing. No one. Even the master screenwriters struggle and miss from time to time, because it's so infinite in it's variations. It's about human nature and our perception of the world around us, so it's inexhaustible.

What "Milagro" was about was the power of an idea, the power of a fictitious character, how some fictitious characters are more real than real people. It's fascinating. There are fictitious characters—I would say any number of the characters created by William Shakespeare, and dozens of others, Sherlock Holmes, for instance—who never lived, but they might as well have, for the impact they've had on history. They're such powerful ideas that they influence people more than millions of people who really did live.

That's what that episode was about. It was about the power of this guy's imagination. Joseph Campbell[21] said that people need stories to survive—not that they like stories to survive, not that they want stories to survive, but you *need* stories to survive. You need narratives because they help you make sense of the world around you, and that's another thing that I think is in that episode: the need for stories.

---

[21] Joseph Campbell (1904–87) was a writer and lecturer best known for his works on mythology, religion, and their influence on storytelling throughout human history.

What was the toughest episode for you to write in your eight years on the show?
There were so many that were so hard. That's one of the nice things about human nature, that you tend to forget the pain and just remember the good things. It was a really hard series, and it was sort of a normal state to feel like it was just absolutely exhausting and very, very difficult. I can't think of a script that was easy; they were all hard in different degrees.

Can you think of any particular plot points that were hurdles you had to surmount?
The one that always stands out—because I can't believe how successful it ended up being—was "Momento Mori," in season four. It was the Scully cancer episode that Chris Carter, Vince Gilligan, John Shiban, and I got nominated for an Emmy for writing.

The reason it sticks out for me is because it was actually going to be a Darin Morgan script. Darin had left the show [at the end of season three], but was going to contribute an episode. Only a week before prep, Darin called and said, "I'm very sorry, but I'm not going to be able to finish the script. I just can't figure it out."

We had to rush and come up with a new episode. We'd contemplated giving Scully cancer that year, but we hadn't yet decided when to do it. We said, "Well, this is going to be the episode," and I think, in about a day and a half, Vince, John, and I boarded that episode, broke that story. Then we each wrote an act in a day, and were able to prep that script before Chris's vacation. Over the vacation, Chris took all of our separate acts and rewrote them into one whole script. That's why it has four writers on it.

To my mind, it's probably the single best mythology episode we did all nine years. It's kind of remarkable, considering how it all came together.

When you were writing the tv series, how many hours a day did you write?
My job was atypical because I was producing the show and usually running the writers' room as well. When I was the writer of an episode, I would typically write [in the] early morning. I would get up at 5:30, and write for two and a half hours before I went to the office. Then, often I would not have the opportunity to write again until night—7:30 or eight o'clock at night—because I had so many other story and producing responsibilities. Very, very rarely would I say, "I'm not available today to do anything else; I'm going to just go and closet myself."

Usually, when I was writing an episode, it would be early morning/late night and weekends; that's how I managed to write almost all of the scripts I wrote.

How did you learn to run the writers' room?
It was one of the blessings of *The X-Files* that Chris had really no respect for titles; it was a meritocracy. At least, from my point of view, it was. Whoever had the best [idea] was free to speak up.

From the very beginning, as an entry-level staff writer, I was in the story meetings because all the doors were open and I just had a feel for it. I had a sense of what should happen, and it became clear very quickly that I was useful in the writers' room.

After three years, I was a co-executive producer on the show, and it just evolved because I had a sense of it. *X-Files* was exactly the kind of show I would have loved as a kid. It was exactly what I would have watched, and I felt it, emotionally as well as intellectually. That's always a gift in the writers' room, when you've got somebody who is connected to what you're doing and can save you literally days of work by coming up with an idea quickly that is a good idea.

That's always the mystery of it to me, why it has to take so long. It's like this process of breaking rocks looking for specs of gold. You know if only you could break those rocks faster, but it takes what it takes sometimes. Anyway, it was just something I had a feel for, and I got the responsibility to match my enthusiasm.

Were you involved in hiring writers?
Yeah. It was always tough hiring writers for the show because there aren't many series on television—especially then—that were in this genre at all. Most writing samples, especially then, were cop shows, lawyer shows, doctor shows.

As good as those series are—and many of them are quite excellent—they're not about what *The X-Files* is about. They're not about supernatural events. They're not idea-driven in the way that genre storytelling tends to be. They weren't cinematic, usually; most of those shows are people talking. It's really good talking, but they're largely about talking.

We increasingly would cast the net wider, and look for people who had been writing features that were sick of the movie business and wanted to try their hand at television. We had a lot of success that way. That's how we got guys like Steve Maeda and Jeff Bell; for both of them, we were their first jobs in television.[22]

Was there anything particular you looked for when reading potential writers?

I hate to read scripts. I have to say, I really do. I helped support myself

---

[22] Steven Maeda was hired for the staff of Chris Carter's *Harsh Realm* (1999). When that series was cancelled after only three episodes, he joined *The X-Files* for it's last three seasons. Over the next decade, he wrote for *CSI: Miami* (2002–5), *Lost* (2005–6), *Day Break* (with Jeffrey Bell, 2006–7), *Lie to Me* (2009), *Miami Medical* and *The Forgotten* (both 2010), *Pan Am* (2011–2), and *Unforgettable* (2012). Most recently, he served as the showrunner for Syfy's *Helix* (2014–5).

Jeffrey Bell joined *The X-Files* in season six, after writing and directing the feature film *Radio Inside* (1994). He stayed with *The X-Files* through season eight, before moving to *Angel* in 2001, where he became the showrunner after the departure of co-creator David Greenwalt. After co-writing and directing the *Angel* finale in 2004, Bell wrote and produced *Alias* (2005–6), *Day Break* (2006–7), *Harper's Island* and *V* (both 2009), created *The Protector* (2011), wrote and produced *Spartacus: War of the Damned* (2013), *Marvel's Agents of S.H.I.E.L.D.* (2013–5), and—as of January 2015—has written (with *Day Break* creator Paul Zbyszewski) the pilot for *Marvel's Most Wanted*.

Jeff Bell also took pity on an ignorant Texan intern—who couldn't figure out how to get from the Fox lot back to his apartment in Burbank in less than two hours—and drew a very helpful map that saved the young man a lot of time.

through film school by reading scripts, by covering them. I would read ten to twelve scripts a week, just to pay my bills.

That must have been miserable…
It is. You realize when you read that many scripts how rare it is to find a really good one. You're so grateful when you get a really good one.

I look for somebody who had control of their narrative, who knew the story they wanted to tell, and—hopefully—it was an engaging story. I don't mean to sound harsh about it, because I think most of my early scripts were pretty dreadful as well.

I've always thought writing is an act of faith; I think very, very few people start out as good writers. Most people start out as pretty bad writers, but if you have faith in yourself, if you keep at it, that muscle will get stronger. Usually, it does if you're motivated to keep looking at yourself and figure out what you're doing wrong.

Did you ever suffer from writer's block?
I never did. I think I was helped in that regard because my previous career was as a wire-service reporter. This was pre-internet, but you were still on a 24-hour deadline because it was the wire service, so I had to—as a reporter—gather information, synthesize it, and write very, very quickly. That was excellent training, as it turned out, for television writing.

You never suffered a loss of the flow of ideas?
No. I've certainly gotten stuck on problems, alluding to what I was

talking about before in the writers' room, where it's like "There is a problem; how do you solve it?" I don't consider that writer's block, though. That's just being stuck.

Do you recall any stories or scripts that just didn't work out and were abandoned?
There are a number of episodes [where] we worked on the stories for weeks, and they never got made. Sometimes, there's an idea that you really liked, that you just find that there's nowhere to go with it. That happened more than once. I've forgotten most of them.

I remember there was one that I really liked, that we worked on more than once and never cracked. It was about a guy who had died and come back, but he remembered death and knew that while he was dead, he'd gone to hell. It changed his view of the world; he knew there was a god, he knew there was a devil, and he knew where he was going. I thought that's such an interesting idea, but we could never find anywhere to go with it. It seemed like the most interesting part of the idea was the beginning, and that was one that frustrated us for weeks.

Are there any stories you'd like to take another crack at if you had the chance to go back in time?
Not really. *The X-Files* was hugely ambitious, so when we succeeded, I think we really succeeded spectacularly. When we failed, they were pretty dreadful.

I'm always surprised by episodes that are not my favorites—I don't want to single them out, because I don't want to hurt anybody's feelings—but I'll meet people who love them. Ones [where] I thought "Boy, we *really* missed that one," I'll meet people...sometimes, it's one of their favorites. You never know what people are going to connect to.

I can't say I want to go back, because every time—I really can say this, and it's one of the things I'm proud of—I really did work as hard as I could to make it as good as I could. That's something I think I learned doing the show for so many years: the value of a good work ethic, that discipline and dedication and never relaxing, never settling back, always pushing yourself to do the best job you can.

It's interesting, when you do that, it gives you a return. You get this—I hate to say—spiritual lift. You feel renewed by the work, and if you ever flag, if you ever start to not try so hard, the opposite effect happens: you start to feel depressed and bad about what you're doing. That's one thing I've tried to carry with me since *The X-Files*, that work ethic.

Was the dismantling of some of the mythology in the first feature film due to it getting out of hand or becoming too convoluted?
The mythology became very complicated, and what you saw was our desire to close down branches of it.

We were discovering—as we were going along—that you get multiple audiences for your show. You get audiences that are very casually interested, who watch maybe one out of every four episodes, but still consider themselves fans. Then you get audiences that have different levels of devotion, and some people knew the mythology episodes as well or better than we did. They're asking very detailed and specific questions that we either hadn't answered or perhaps we'd answered but there was some ambiguity to those answers.

You realized that it became impossible to satisfy all those audiences. You can't hope to answer all the questions of the die-hard mythology fan without boring or alienating the much larger audience that isn't paying such close attention. That became increasingly challenging as the show went on.

To me, the hardest thing, though, was not just the complexity of the mythology as the show got older, but that we didn't know when we were going to wrap up. In both season seven and eight, we had to write and film the season finales without knowing whether they were the *series* finales, so you can imagine how difficult that was. We had to say, well, okay, if this is the end of the show, that's going to be a really good ending...but if it's not, we have to be ready to go on for another season. That was really, really tough. That was the hardest part.

We found ways to sort of narrow [the mythology] for ourselves. A lot of people still don't realize it or believe it, but [in] season seven, Mulder came to the conclusion that his sister was dead. There's an episode called "Closure" where he actually believes his sister is dead and it was really fortuitous that we did that because David ended up leaving; that was his last full-time season.

When we had Scully get pregnant, that was certainly a narrowing of our options; that really sent the mythology in a certain direction that we had to pursue.

I think we made some pretty smart decisions, looking back at it, about how to keep the mythology manageable in the later years.

Did you decide—at the moment the writers impregnated Scully—that it was going to be Mulder's child, or was that decided later on?
No, we knew it was going to be Mulder's kid. We planted a moment—excuse the wording—in the episode that Gillian Anderson wrote and directed ["all things"], which people could look back on and realize *that* was the night that they conceived. We planned for it, anticipated it.

We also intended to withhold telling the audience whether it was Mulder's baby for as long as possible. When we finally did tell the audience it was Mulder's baby, even that [was] worded so ambiguously that a lot of people weren't sure. I still get asked, "Is it Mulder's baby?" *Yes*, it is Mulder's baby.

You explicitly laid out that it was Mulder's baby in one of the DVD commentaries, and it was clear that you'd been asked that question too many times.
Yeah, although I've started to forget as time's gone on. When the show was on the air, or right after it was gone off the air, I could remember everything—about the mythology, every episode, every actor, every title—it was all in my head. As time goes, you start to discard a lot of that information, because you know you just don't need it anymore.

What were the challenges in introducing Doggett and Reyes as the new leads of the show?
As you can imagine, huge. Enormous. I really wasn't at all convinced it

was a good idea to even attempt it, because it's hard in any series to change horses, but especially hard in a series like this because it was defined by Mulder's quest. Scully was equally the lead with Mulder, but it was his quest; he was the believer. He was the one whose sister had been lost. To go on without him seemed almost impossible.

We knew the audience was going to be hostile to this whole idea. They loved David Duchovny, they loved Mulder. The last thing they wanted was [for] some interloper to come in, so the first thing we decided to do [was to have] Scully be the agent of that hostility. In the first episodes where Robert Patrick appears as John Doggett, Scully hates him; the audience is able to vicariously vent their dislike of anybody new through Scully. What was really successful about it was he was having to respond to her hatred and he did it so gracefully—in such a winning way—that he won her over, and in the process he won over the audience as well.

This has sort of been lost in the conventional wisdom, since the show went off the air, but the ratings actually went up for season eight, which was the first season without David full-time; we increased our audience. That's a testament to Robert Patrick, and how great he was in the part.

Even though I was really far [from] convinced it was a good idea to go on without David, I ended up having a really great time as a writer in seasons eight and nine because it was a whole new set of problems to solve, and we had these wonderful new actors to work with. It was a new challenge.

Then, season nine…who knows what happened in season nine? I think there were a lot of people who were not going to like seasons eight and nine no matter what because Mulder had left. It didn't really matter what we wrote or shot, they just weren't going to like the show.

Objectively speaking, we did episodes that were as good as anything we'd ever done in seasons eight and nine. The quality didn't decrease in the least, but [in] season nine, something strange happened—a section of the audience simply didn't come back. We were still a highly rated show. We were still doing well enough, but it was not nearly as big an audience as we'd had the previous year.

Two Sundays after 9/11, I remember picking up the Sunday *New York Times* magazine, and they had a chart that said things that are "in" and things that are "out" after 9/11; *The X-Files* was one of the things that was out. I remember looking at that and thinking what are they talking about? Why would we be out after 9/11? Government conspiracy? That's only part of the show, that's not going to…

In the months and the years since then I've come to believe that was a big part of what happened in season nine, that things in *The X-Files* didn't feel fun anymore, in that immediate, post-9/11 atmosphere. That was a big factor in why there were fewer viewers in that season than there had been previously.

Why do you think now is the right time for a second *X-Files* film?
I don't know if it is. I hope it is, I guess, because we're making it now. It was never our intention to wait this long. It happened because of this lawsuit between Chris and the studio over profits from the tv series, but

I think—in some ways—it's been fortuitous. The long absence has given us a lot to say, a lot to write about. Mulder and Scully are not the same people they were six years ago, and that made it very interesting for us as writers. I hope will make it very interesting for the audience.

It's also given people time to miss the characters, and miss the show. I definitely feel that. I feel a lot of affection from people for the series, which has been really nice, and a lot of enthusiasm for the movie.

Finally, I think you could say the show ended in the post-9/11 climate. I think we're in a post-post-9/11 climate now. We've moved beyond that mood that the country was in when *The X-Files* first came to an end. I think those are all things that are encouraging for the audience.

How has the Spotnitz/Carter collaboration altered in the absence of writing together for six years?
It hasn't really at all. In fact, we had written a script together only a year and a half before, for Paramount, that has not been made.[23] We never stopped speaking to each other; I think we spoke probably every week, or more, in all those years.

The collaboration is, I'd say, exactly the same. We're certainly older, though. We have different concerns than we did six years ago, and I think that informed our depiction of Mulder and Scully's relationship and where they are in their lives. I was really struck, coming back to

---

[23] In 2004, Carter and Spotnitz were hired to adapt and produced—with Carter directing—a feature film version of Phillip Kerr's 1992 novel A PHILOSOPHICAL INVESTIGATION. As of March 2016, the movie has not been made.

them, by how much they've been through; they're characters who bear a lot of scars. [It's] not surprising—given the genre we're writing, the supernatural genre—but I mean the emotional scars. They've been through a lot, and I'm moved by them in a deeper way than I was before.

What is the process when you and Chris work on a script together?
We've done it all different ways in the past. Sometimes we've literally been in the room together with one of us at the keyboard typing and both of us talking and putting it down. Other times, I'll write an act or even a draft, and then Chris will rewrite it. Then I'll go [over it again]; it's not so much rewriting his rewrites, but giving him notes.

In this instance, we were not in the same place, so Chris would write and send me sections of the script. I would react to what he had done. I wouldn't call it rewriting so much as going through it scene by scene, and bouncing the file back to him. Then he would bounce the file back to me, and we did that sort of ping-pong with the file endlessly. That was sort of the writing process with the script.

Is it true that the plot for *I Want to Believe* was conceived at the end of the series, but that the story was lost during the intervening legal issues?
Yeah. I'll give you the whole blow-by-blow.

[Fox] came to us before the series ended to do the movie; they actually came to us in 2001. At that time, we were still doing the show, so we didn't work on it. The show ended in 2002, and we felt like we needed a break. I think it was early 2003 when we said, "Okay, let's sit down and figure out what the story for the movie would be." We came up with this story, and we pitched it to the studio and they said, "Great." Then the deal making started, and then the lawsuit, and then nothing happened.

It stayed like that—completely stalled—until early 2007 when Chris's issues with the studio were settled, and suddenly we were back on.

In that four-year period, we had misplaced all the [index] cards we had written about this story; we couldn't find them at all. We still remembered pretty clearly what the story was, but we didn't actually have the specific details that we worked out, so we had to start over.

I think it was just fine, honestly. While the x-file—the case—is the same as it was in 2003, everything else about the movie changed because, after the passage of so much time, we realized that Mulder and Scully would be in very different places in their lives. What their story was about, what their emotion journey would be, had changed completely. It wasn't as big of a loss as it sounds.

Has the same amount of time elapsed in Mulder and Scully's lives, as it has in real time, since the series ended?
That's exactly right: six years later.

Is the movie a stand-alone story rather than a mythology tale?
Yeah. The first movie pretty much had to be a mythology [story]. There was huge demand for it to be that. This time, we didn't feel like we had

to do that, and we didn't want to do that. It's more like what most of the tv show was, which is a scary, stand-alone investigation.

What's different about [this] movie than the tv show is that the characters of Mulder and Scully are really front and center; it's very much about them—who they are, and what the nature of their relationship is—in a way that you couldn't do on television week in, week out. You have to be a little stingier in tv, because you've got twenty-four hours [per season] and you can only do so much in their personal lives without exhausting the audience. [*I Want to Believe*] is a more intimate, personal story than we usually were able to do on television.

Did the studio have a lot of notes on the movie script?
I wouldn't say they had a lot of notes. I think they had strategic notes that were pretty uniformly excellent. That was one of the pleasures of doing this movie really from beginning to end, that the studio saw it the same way we did. From the very beginning, doing it as a stand-alone, smaller film was their desire and ours—from pitching the story to the first draft, we all wanted to make the same film. That's a real advantage, because, frequently, when you're developing a movie, the writer or writers want one thing and the studio wants something else; that just was never the case here.

Can you give me an example of the notes that the studio gave?
Sharpening conflict, making clear what's the conflict between Mulder and Scully in certain instances. What are the objectives of the bad guys in certain instances. Ideas for a clue here and there.

It was all very helpful and constructive and smart, and it really made it as painless a process as can be.

Why was there a desire on everyone's part to go with a smaller film?
I think we wanted to do something really creepy and scary and intimate. That's the aesthetic of *The X-Files*: the more real, the scarier it will seem; that's always been our belief.

As much as I love these big-budget, visual-effects driven movies, they don't usually feel very much like real life; they usually feel like departures from real life. It didn't make sense—given the type of story we wanted to tell—to take that kind of big-budget, visual-effects kind of approach.

Can you speak to the nature of Mulder and Scully's relationship as the movie opens?
My lips are sealed. I can't.

What did you learn from making *Fight the Future* that you employed in writing *I Want to Believe*?
This movie is not as physically ambitious as the first film. It's not a giant production, it's smaller scale, more reality based. The thing I learned from the first movie was that, while we liked to say that we're doing a little movie every week at *The X-Files*, we really weren't. When you do a movie, because you have more time, you film more—you film more angles—so it gives you far more choices editorially, far more ways to go. It becomes a much more complex process.

The complexity of doing a movie is greater than the complexity of doing a television show, simply because of the amount of time and money you're given.

Were you able to be on set during the production?
I was. For all the years we did television shows in Vancouver, I used to go up and visit. I'd go for the last few days of prep, then come home.

This time, I was in Vancouver for three or four months. I'd fly home every weekend as best I could, to see my family and they'd come up to see me, but I'd never spent so much sustained time in Vancouver as I did this time. It's a wonderful city with very warm people, and we had an incredible crew. It was a real treat to spend time there.

Did *I Want to Believe*'s script evolve much during production, or did it stay as you'd written it at the outset?
It had to stay exactly as we'd written it, because the writers' strike began right after we'd got the green light, days after we'd got the green light. Since the writers in this case were the producers, we thought the script was in pretty good shape. It didn't bother us in the least, so we didn't change a word.

Is it harder to keep a movie like this secret now than it was in the early days of the internet when *The X-Files* began?
It is so much harder to keep anything secret now than it has ever been before. All it takes is one person to find out, and then it's all over the world in a matter of seconds. You can't put the cork back in the bottle once it has been opened, so it's very, very challenging.

I think the net effect is very positive, because you have fans talking to each other all over the world, and this real community that's very excited. Every day I'm getting emails from Russia and Brazil and Germany and Italy and all over the United States. It's incredible how connected *X-Files* fans can be.

In terms of showmanship, for us, this is a very unique situation because we've been away for six years and so there's a lot of questions that people want answered. We think there's value in saving those answers for opening night. It's the element of surprise that you can never have twice, and there's a lot more power in experiencing those surprises in a movie theater than reading them online, as obvious as it sounds.

There're a lot of people with time on their hands, and it's sport for them to try and puncture these balloons, try and uncover these secrets. We've worked very hard to keep it a secret, and you have to be proactive about it. On the one hand, we took extraordinary security measures with the script. I think it made production even more challenging, because so few people on our crew were even allowed to read the script. Most of the people working on the movie didn't even know what the movie was about. They'd go to work and do their jobs, not knowing what was going to happen in the story each day.

But it's more than that. You have to go online, and you have to be proactive about muddying the water, because it's the only way to keep people from finding out what you're up to.

You're saying that you have a campaign of disinformation.
Yes, we have. We've done some things to mislead and...all in the spirit of love, because we were just trying to protect the movie.

I'd have to say we've had an awful lot of help. The very few things we've done have been amplified and added to and there've been plenty of other people on [the internet]—for whatever reason—spreading all kinds of disinformation that has nothing to do with us.

When you look at the 2008 tv landscape, what influence do you see from *The X-Files*?
I don't know. People tell me they think *The X-Files* influenced *Lost* and *Heroes*, and other shows. [I] would like to think that's true. I'd be very proud to have that be true, but I don't know. It's hard for me to judge.

The thing I'm proudest of is that people still know *The X-Files*, care about it. I still hear from people who've only recently started watching it, and that's great because we always hoped—when we were doing the show—that it have a shelf life; we never thought this was just something to put on the air Friday or Sunday and then be done with. We were always aiming for longevity, and it's gratifying that it's lasted this long.

Today's viewers can watch and be astonished by the size of 1993 cell phones.
Exactly. We were making that joke even when the show was on the air. We did a flashback episode ["Unusual Suspects," set in 1989] at the beginning of season five, where Mulder met the Lone Gunmen for the

first time, and he pulls a cell phone out of his suit. It's the size of his shoe. That was a joke we saw coming.

VINCE GILLIGAN
16 June 2008

How did you become interested in screenwriting?
I was always interested in making movies. In third grade, I had a wonderful elementary school art teacher who let me borrow her Super 8 movie camera over summer vacation. I would make little science fiction movies starring my younger brother. I always loved movies.

Back then, I didn't differentiate between writing and directing and doing the special effects; it was a labor of love in which you did everything. I came to realize—as the years went by—that my talents lay in writing. That's how it started, back in third grade.

How did you transition from Super 8 filmmaker to screenwriter?
I got very lucky. I went to NYU film school, and studied film production there. I wrote a movie script for a senior thesis class in screenwriting. I entered it in a screenwriting contest in my home state of Virginia, back in 1989. I was one of the winners that year.

One of the judges was a producer named Mark Johnson. He was judging at that small Virginia contest on account of he'd been a student years before at the University of Virginia. He was doing them a favor as an alumnus. He read the script, really liked it, and called me after the competition was over. He said, "Do you have any other scripts?" I've been working with him ever since, and he's now an executive producer along with me on *Breaking Bad*. I've been working with him going on twenty years, based on that meeting.

Didn't Johnson produced *Wilder Napalm*, your first movie?[24]
Yes, and he produced *Home Fries*,[25] and he's produced [*Breaking Bad*], and an ill-fated pilot we did for CBS that never went anywhere.[26] We were steadily trying to get movies made—and later tv series—for twenty years now. He's my mentor in the business.

Why did you make the move from movies to television?
I had an agent whose assistant was a real up-and-coming young guy on his way to becoming an agent; [he] suggested that I move into television.

---

[24] *Wilder Napalm* (1993) was directed by Glenn Gordon Caron (creator of *Moonlighting* and *Medium*), and starred Dennis Quaid and Arliss Howard as a pair of pyrokinetic brothers in a love triangle.

[25] *Home Fries* (1998) was directed by Dean Parisot (*Galaxy Quest*), and starred Drew Barrymore as a pregnant woman who unwittingly falls in love with the stepson of her baby's late father.

[26] See page 88, for more on this "pilot…that never went anywhere."

He's Chris Silberman, now one of the heads of ICM. He's a good guy to listen to; he knows what he's talking about. When I first met him, he was a lowly assistant, as it were. Within just a few short years, he was a big, star agent, and now he's one of the guys running ICM. I can't believe it, looking back on it; it seems like yesterday.

How did you find yourself on Chris Carter's radar?
I was living in Virginia, trying to make a living writing movie scripts when *The X-Files* came on. I watched the very first episode. I happened to be home on Friday night, turned on the tv, and I didn't have cable at the time, otherwise I might have missed it. I thought, man, this show is *good*. I love this thing. I became very much a fan of it, and watched every week from that point onward.

I was talking to my agent six months into the show—we were talking about other business—and, apropos of nothing, I said to her "Have you seen *The X-Files*? It's really good."

She said, "As a matter of fact, I'm related to the guy who created it by marriage." She was some first or second cousin to [Chris's] wife. That's how Hollywood works, I guess: nepotism and who you know! My agent said, "Would you like to meet Chris Carter next time you're out on movie business in California?"

I said, "Well, sure. I'd love to shake his hand and tell him how much I love his show." At this point, the show was not the phenomenon it later became; it was well-respected, but not widely viewed.

I was on movie business, out in Los Angeles, and true to her word, [my agent] set up a meeting for me with Chris. I was just looking to shake his hand and congratulate him. I was not looking to get a job on the show because I considered myself a movie writer. I wasn't at all snobbish about tv; I knew that writing tv entailed moving to Los Angeles, and I really liked my little house in Virginia, where everything is cheaper and the tax rate is lower, and all my family is back there.

[Chris] said to me, "Do you have any ideas for an episode?" I'd had an idea the night before in the hotel, looking at my shadow on the wall as I was watching tv, and I thought about how creepy it would be if it suddenly started moving independently of me. Not the most original thought in the world, but I pitched that to him and we kind of spitballed it for a little bit.

Lo and behold, they hired me to write it as a freelance one-off.[27] I was suddenly very excited. I figured it would be a one-time thing, but very fortunately for me, it led to me becoming a member of the staff, which was the best single thing that ever did happen to me.

It taught me so much about writing that I thought I knew but I didn't. Being on a tv staff, with other really talented people, Chris Carter being chief amongst them, you can't help but learn from being in that environment. You become a better writer, and you learn to be a producer when you're on a writing staff of a tv show. If the executive producer

---

[27] "Soft Light" was Gilligan's first contribution to *The X-Files*, toward the end of season two. He joined the series as a staff writer midway through the following season.

allows you any kind of responsibility at all on your episode, you learn to become a producer. That job was the single greatest job I ever had, and I kind of fell into it. I kinda think of myself as Kramer from *Seinfeld*, falling ass-backward into good luck.

What did you learn in your early days of working for Chris Carter?
I learned the realities of doing television. When I wrote that first episode, "Soft Light," my first draft of that thing was a shadow that moved independently of its owner and it sucked people in like a black hole. I had a huge act four action sequence that was—looking back on it—laughable. The budget back then on *The X-Files* was maybe $2.5 million an episode, and this first draft would have cost probably $20 million to make. I learned the realities of doing it for a budget and on a tight schedule. I learned that very quickly.

[Television] was a mystery to me. I was so naïve when I got that first *X-Files* job—I'm embarrassed to say this now, but it's true—when I watched those early episodes, and the title came up and it said RICHMOND, VIRGINIA or OTTUMWA, IOWA, or wherever they'd be story-wise doing their investigation, I thought they actually went to those places. Pretty sad to admit, but it's true. I thought maybe they sent a little crew out and get that stuff. Suffice to say, I learned a lot in a few short months that first season I was a staff member.

How did the Ten Thirteen style of boarding a story differ from how you wrote your movies?
When I wrote those previous movie scripts—before I had *The X-Files* training—I would just fill those old black-and-white composition

books they give you in high school. I'd buy a bunch of those, and fill them up with notes. I would write outlines in longhand. Invariably, I'd get kind of bored with outlining—I'd be itching to write because I had a lot of good stuff for the opening scene and for the second act—and before I'd figure out the ending of the movie, I'd just start writing. I'd figure the ending would take care of itself, and that's why I had a lot of act three problems in those early movies.

Everyone's career and everyone's way of working's—in my mind—kind of like a snowflake; there's no two that are completely alike. Having said that, I need structure. I need to know where I'm going; I need road maps, a plan to get from point A to point Z at the end of the script. That was a big failing on my part, early on. I just figured I'll find it when I find it.

The X-Files taught me that you're not ready to start writing until you know what happens right before you type in The End. You need to have the whole thing in your head before you start. In a way, it liberates you. It doesn't lock you up. It doesn't make it less creative. To my way of thinking, it makes you more creative because it allows you to know where you're going in the back of your mind. Then, you have the fun of dotting all the is and crossing all the ts, and putting in all the small details that get you from start to finish.

Do you still use the same process on *Breaking Bad*?
Yes, that boarding process—where we card every plot point on an index card, which I learned on *The X-Files*—I still use on *Breaking Bad*. As a matter of fact, my writing staff now laughs at me because they think I'm

kind of obsessive compulsive with it; it's good natured laughing, but they laugh at me nonetheless.

It's right down to the way Chris did it. We use a specific kind of Sharpie, and we squash the end of the new Sharpie down so it's just thick enough for the boldness of the line. The lettering has to be as perfect as we can make it, and you can't have words get all squashy at the end of the card, as if you're trying to fit too much in. The line of cards—with the thumbtacks in them—has to be perfectly level. It's a little OCD. It's a little ritual. You need those rituals, whatever it takes to get you in your comfort zone to get the writing done efficiently and quickly.

I think rituals are important. I'm not a big sports guy, but you see 'em in baseball. You see the ritual that the pitcher does before he throws his fast ball; he's gotta tap his heel twice and whatever he does. It's sort of akin to that.

Have you ever suffered from writer's block, and if so, how did you overcome it?
That's a phrase you don't even like to say out loud, because you don't want to tempt it.

That's the beauty of having a writing staff, a bunch of really smart, enthusiastic people in the room with you. If you're having a slow day or a day in which the creative juices just aren't flowing, you have other people in the room who are hopefully having a better day than you. They pull you through it.

There were days when nothing much happened in the room. I wouldn't call it writer's block. Everyone has hours or days—or maybe a week straight—where the ideas just aren't coming, but writer's block feels like a thing born of anxiety. We had anxiety all throughout, the anxiety of the schedule we had to make; we were running for our lives the whole season long, to the point where we didn't have time for anxiety to shut us down. We didn't want to lose our jobs and be out of work.

The short answer is, luckily, no writer's block; there just wasn't time.

If you started feeling that way, I think you tell yourself, "It's only a movie. It's only a tv show. It's not a cure for cancer; people won't live or die based on the plot decisions you make right now, so go ahead and make some." That's the way I've found to look at it: it's not earth-shatteringly important, so go ahead and put something on the page. You can always change it later.

How did "Pusher" come about?
It came about the way they all came about, you sit around and you sort of noodle ideas.

Come to think about it, I cannibalized the starting point of that episode from a movie script I had written the summer before that never went anywhere. It was like a weird cross between a UFO- and an *Ocean's Eleven*-type story: a bunch of guys based out of Nellis Air Force Base in Nevada use this Cold War technology to cover up a big casino rip off by making it look like it was some sort of UFO thing. It was kind of a mishmash of ideas, and it never got made.

I had this idea at the tail end of it—a little bit of a *Manchurian Candidate*-kind of thing—where there's a code word that one character says to the other. It was "cerulean," and when the guy had that word put into his head, it made him drive in front of a truck. I remembered that, and nobody really liked [this movie script] anyway, so I cannibalized that bit. What if—just with a word—someone could make you do anything he wanted you to do, no matter if it was self-destructive or against your best interest?

As soon as I had that idea, it all started falling together. It takes a while to get the plot figured out to its best effect, but that big idea was very exciting to me and intriguing, that idea of someone could impose his will upon you. I guess that's where that one came from.

Do you think your season four serial killer-centric stories (and serial sex offender story, in the case of "Small Potatoes") were a side effect of *Millennium*[28] being in production at the same time?
Maybe. It might have been in the air. I can't remember when I read the [*Millennium*] pilot. I know Chris disappeared for a little while when he was working on that pilot. When we finally read it, we were all really impressed with it.

---

[28] *Millennium* (1996–9) was Chris Carter's first series created and produced after the success of *The X-Files*. It centered on Frank Black (Lance Henriksen), a former FBI profiler and consultant for the mysterious Millennium Group, who had a gift for getting inside the minds of serial killers. When the series was cancelled a year before the turn of the "popular millennium" in 2000, Vince Gilligan and Frank Spotnitz wrote an episode of *The X-Files* the following season—titled "Millennium"—which sought to provide closure for Frank Black, with assistance from Mulder and Scully.

An x-file's a tricky thing because you had to have the supernatural element of it—the paranormal element of it—but you also had to have the legitimate FBI investigation, which nine times out of ten means you gotta have a crime of some sort. You wanted to keep it exciting and nail-biting, and I guess, in those seasons, maybe [serial killing] was in the air.

You were one of the few writers to use Mulder's psychology background after the pilot. What intrigued you about that?
I like building on what we already know about a character. We do that to a ridiculous extent on *Breaking Bad*.

There're two kinds of series. There's the series where it's a little island of a story and the characters don't change that much from week to week. Then the other kind of a series is serialized, and moves forward. The little island series, on the whole, are easier to write. At this moment in time, I'd kind of prefer to be doing something like that a little more, because the serialization of *Breaking Bad* is kind of killing us, but in a good way! We're excited to be doing what we're doing.

I tend toward the idea of making tv shows as much like real life as you possibly can. If Agent Mulder gets whacked in the head in episode three, maybe he's getting headaches in episode six.

It's just the nature of television—a lot of tv shows do this—but we often had episodes where Mulder or Scully would get shot, and in the next episode they're fine. That worked for me. That still works for me, as a viewer. It's a little bit of poetic license. You have to see it as, "I don't know how the two [episodes] were related time-wise. Just because I watched the one [episode] one week and the next [episode] the next week doesn't mean that—in their world—[those two episodes] are a week apart. It's the same way the funny pages work, Charlie Brown and the *Family Circus* never seems to grow up; they're sort of frozen in time.

I respond more to the serialized way of telling stories, even though it's often harder. You've got to be very careful not to write yourself into a corner.

Starting with "Small Potatoes," how did you become the go-to guy for *X-Files* episodes in a more comedic vein?
Darin Morgan was the first guy to write a comedic episode. He was an extraordinarily funny guy, and really great writer. He'd left the writing staff at that point. If he had remained there, he would have been the guy doing those, but he had left the show.[29]

I started off writing comedy movie scripts, and when I got *The X-Files* job, I worried that I wasn't going to be able to do it because I'd never done straight drama before. I'd never done horror and all that kind of stuff, I naturally tend more toward comedy.

I had written a few episodes that had worked out pretty well, and I

---

[29] Darin Morgan was a staff writer during season three of *The X-Files*, winning the 1996 Primetime Emmy Award for Outstanding Writing for a Drama Series with his script "Clyde Bruckman's Final Repose." Morgan returned to *The X-Files* to play the part of Eddie Van Blundht in "Small Potatoes," and later wrote and directed two season two episodes of Chris Carter's *Millennium*. He returned to write and direct an episode of the 2016 revival of *The X-Files*.

seemed to be in a pretty safe place on the staff at the point. I went to Chris and said, "Can I write a funny one?" I'm glad he let me do it. I wouldn't do it every single time out, because *The X-Files* had to be more serious than funny, but every third or fourth one, I would say, "Can I do another funny one now?" They worked out pretty well, so Chris let me.

I wasn't the only one to do them. I certainly wasn't the first, and I wasn't the last either. Jeff Bell wrote a really funny episode called "Rain King," and he did a really great job with that one.

It was fun to get to do those. They were just as hard to plot, but they were more fun to write, on the whole.

How did you land the job of putting The Lone Gunmen[30] in the spotlight for "The Unusual Suspects?"
David and Gillian were not available for one episode because they were finishing up shooting [the first] movie. We sat around, all of us, thinking out loud, saying "What the hell are we going to do? How do you do an *X-Files* episode without Mulder or Scully?"

In the past, we had gotten rid of Gillian for an episode or two when she was pregnant in real life, but this was a new one on us. I can't remember whose idea it was, but one of us had the idea about the Lone Gunmen.

---

[30] The Lone Gunmen were: John Fitzgerald Byers (Bruce Harwood), Melvin Frohike (*The X-Files*'s Assistant Director Tom Braidwood), and Richard "Ringo" Langly (Dean Haglund).

I got to be the guy to write it, which thrilled me because I always loved the Lone Gunmen. I'm so glad Glen Morgan and James Wong created those guys, because they're my favorite to write for in the whole series.

The first board we had for that episode was something I'd come up with with John Shiban and Frank Spotnitz. We pitched it to Chris, and he wasn't mean about it, but he politely picked it to pieces. It was the only time ever we left with nothing. He said, "I don't think any of this works," and he was right.

It was an episode with nanotechnology. It would have been, in a sense, the first episode of what became *The Lone Gunmen* tv show, because it would have been a show where these guys investigate something completely on their own. We're sitting there with Chris, and he's saying, "I don't know if this works," and then he said, "But what if you tell the origin story of how these guys came to be?" As soon as he said that, it was, "Oh, of course! That's a great idea."

It was so much fun coming up with how these guys met, the fact that none of them liked each other at first, and the idea that Byers worked for the government and was so pro-government. It was all because Chris threw out the first board. I'm so glad he did.

Can you recall any stories you worked on that were never produced?
I got real lucky. I was there for seven years and there was nothing. Toward the end, we were running for our lives and we didn't have a cupboard of ideas. Early on, we did. Frank Spotnitz had an idea about a magician he wanted to do for seasons on end. I had an idea I wanted to

do for several seasons straight, a crossover between *The X-Files* and the tv show *Cops*.³¹ We were there so long we got to do all of them. By the time season nine ended, the cupboard was bare. I got to do everything.

I'll reminisce about the show, because I'm kind of nostalgic. It was a great job, and every now and then I'll think, "That would have been a good x-file," but I didn't leave the show with any outstanding [ideas] that I had really hoped to do.

Do you recall an idea for an *Unsolved Mysteries*-style episode?³²
Yeah, vaguely. We talked about that. It never went very far, but, yeah, we wanted to have Robert Stack³³ in an episode because he was the host of that show.

How did "X-Cops" come to be?
That one took several years for me to convince Chris to let me do it. The big sticking point for him was he thought it felt a little gimmicky.

---

³¹ *Cops*, created by John Langley and Malcolm Barbour, is a documentary series that follows police officers on their patrols, chronicling the day-to-day work of law enforcement. The series aired on Fox from 1989–2013. Spike TV has continued it since 2013.

³² *Unsolved Mysteries*, created by John Cosgrove and Terry-Dunn Meurer, was a documentary television series that profiled real-life mysteries, including everything from true crime to paranormal phenomena. *Unsolved Mysteries* was initially hosted by actor Robert Stack, and was broadcast by NBC from 1987–97, CBS from 1997–9, and Lifetime from 2001–2. The series was revived by Spike TV from 2008–10, with Dennis Farina as the host.

³³ Actor Robert Stack (1919–2013) hosted *Unsolved Mysteries* from 1987–2002.

The other thing that really didn't thrill him was the idea that I had for shooting it on video.

He said, "Why don't we just shoot it on film, because film looks better than video?"

I said, "Yes, it sure does, but that's not the point. The point is to make an episode of *Cops*."

To that end, we wound up shooting not just on video, we wound up shooting on the actual Betacam cameras that *Cops* used.[34] We used a couple of their camera men, and we used their tape editor to cut together our initial montage for the title sequence. We had the full cooperation of their whole staff, and of John Langley, the creator of that show. He was a really cool guy. He gave me a cigar on the set one night; that was cool.

That show was an awful lot of fun to do, but I guess I'm glad that was one of the few we did that way. That show, to me, was reality tv, but it's the first of its kind. It's still, to this day, interesting to me. What is now called reality tv is just—it's not the first or last time you're going to hear this—crap. It's just demented. Scripted tv is more real than what passes for "reality" these days.

I shouldn't state that it's all bad. There're probably some really good

---

[34] Unfortunately, the company that re-created *The X-Files* in high definition for the 2015 Blu-ray release of the series did not note that "X-Cops" was produced to mimic the visual aesthetic of *Cops,* and "fixed it."

reality shows. *Project Greenlight*! I'm sorry that's off the air; I really enjoyed that while that was on.[35]

How did directing "Je Souhaite" change your approach to writing?
I don't know that it changed me as a writer, but it changed me. It was a wonderful experience. I was so nervous leading up to it. I had been on the show probably five years at that point, and I had expressed my interest in the idea of directing an episode. Chris was very nice to let me do it. Once he said yes, then I started getting nervous. I was like, "Oh my god, now I've gotta be responsible for $4.5 million of Fox's money and I'm gonna have eighty, ninety, 100 people standing around on a set waiting for me to say something. I hate crowds. I hate being the center of attention. You want your work to be the center of attention, but not you. How am I going to stand there with all these eyes on me and tell everybody what to do?

I had a lot of nightmares in the weeks leading up to it, and a lot of gastric distress. A week or two out, I started weakening. I began to think there's no harm done now if I back out of it gracefully. They'll put another director on it. It'll be fine. Maybe I'm just not ready yet.

I had long talks with my girlfriend, Holly, and she said, "What's the

---

[35] *Project Greenlight*, created by Alex Keledjian, developed by Eli Holzman and produced by Ben Affleck, Matt Damon, Sean Bailey, and Chris Moore, was a documentary series that gave first-time filmmakers an opportunity to write and direct a feature film. The series ran on HBO for two seasons from 2001 to 2003, producing the movies *Stolen Summer* (2002) and *The Battle of Shaker Heights* (2003). Bravo revived the series in 2005, yielding the movie *Feast* (2005). In 2015, Gilligan's desire for the series's resurrection was fulfilled when HBO produced a fourth season.

worst that could happen?" I said, "The worst that could happen is I lose all that money because I shut down on the first day and sit there catatonic." She said, "So what happens then? They put another director on. They bring [director] Kim Manners in, or somebody. Maybe at most they lose 50,000 bucks Fox can stand to lose." She said, in other words, the worst thing that can happen is you get embarrassed. I said, "Yeah." She said, "I think it's worth the risk," and she was right. She was right.[36]

I went ahead, and in that first hour and a half of the first morning, I was scared out of my mind. Leading up to it—getting there at five in the morning and being on the lot—I could hear the trucks in the distance starting up. Being there, and knowing I had to go over in thirty minutes and start acting like a director, that was the scariest time. It's weird, you look back on those scary moments very fondly.

I got on the set that morning and kind of went through it on autopilot for the first hour and a half, and then I started relaxing and about halfway through that first day. I was having such a good time, I realized that—I knew this anyway, but I really truly understood—everybody was there to support the director and to tell a good story. Everybody was happy to be there, and they weren't looking at me like I was an idiot. They were happy to do good work, and it was so much fun. I had such a good time.

---

[36] As of January 2016, Vince Gilligan has been nominated three times for Primetime Emmy Awards for Outstanding Directing for a Drama Series, for the *Breaking Bad* pilot; the fourth-season finale, "Face Off;" and the series finale, "Felina." Holly was *very* right.

It's never good to get scared off of doing something, especially when the only bad thing that can happen is you get scuffed up a bit. You getting embarrassed is not a good reason to not do something.

How did writing *The Lone Gunmen* spinoff[37] differ from scripting the parent series?
We had thirteen episodes [of *The Lone Gunmen*] that season. We had to split our time between *The Lone Gunmen* and *The X-Files*, and it was ridiculously hard.

Right now, on *Breaking Bad*, I have thirteen episodes total. I look back, and I don't know how we did it. Thirteen episodes right now on *Breaking Bad* seems borderline impossible to me, but looking back on it, we had thirteen of *The Lone Gunmen* and we had twenty-two of *The X-Files*; I don't know how it all got done, but somehow it does. You have a finite amount of time, and you figure out a way. One way or the other, you figure a way to get it all done. All the work you need done gets done.

It was a wonderful time. It was hugely stressful and anxiety ridden, with the deadlines we had to continually hit, but I just love writing that show.

---

[37] *The Lone Gunmen* aired on Fox from 4 March to 1 June 2001, alongside season eight of *The X-Files*. The pilot episode—written by Chris Carter, Vince Gilligan, John Shiban, and Frank Spotnitz—concerned a plot to fly a commercial airliner into the World Trade Center, and was broadcast just over seven months before terrorists carried out exactly such a plot on 11 September 2001.

That was my single biggest disappointment during those years, when that show got cancelled at the end of that first season. I truly love that show and it was a real heartbreaker when it ended.

The best way I can put it is I love the movie *Jaws*, and it's not because it's a scary movie or an intense, exciting movie, although it is. What I love about *Jaws* is I want to be on that boat with those three guys; they're just fun guys to be around. That's sort of what I got from the Lone Gunmen; I wanted to hang out with those guys, go to the Red Lobster with them, or hang out and hear them talk shit about computers and try to save the world in their own dopey way.

When you work that intensely, when you write a character for thirteen hours of storytelling for a whole season straight, you spend that much time thinking about these guys, they really do kind of come alive for you. It's as if they're in the room with you. Luckily, I like those guys, because I had to spend an awful lot of time with them. We all did—Frank and John and Chris—we all spent a lot of time with them.

How did writing Doggett and Reyes differ from writing Mulder and Scully?

It was tricky. It was tricky because you want your two characters to have different points of view. Mulder and Scully kind of are the perfect example of that; they had very different points of view. Doggett and Reyes have to have that too, but they also have to be different characters; you don't want just different-looking versions of Mulder and Scully, and they were tough to write, a little tough to pin down.

It's a shame. Those actors were wonderful; Robert Patrick and Annabeth Gish are very talented actors who we were lucky to have working on our show, and it always bothered me that so many folks—fans—piled so much venom on those two. A lot of the folks on the internet saw them as carpetbaggers, as if they had somehow come in and kicked Mulder off the show, as if it had nothing to do with the fact that David Duchovny just no longer wanted to be there and had basically quit on us. [The fans] were taking it out on this poor guy, Robert Patrick, who is really just a marvelous guy and a wonderful actor. He was always a real sport about it, very upbeat about the whole thing.

For a brief period there, I'd read the internet, and I learned to stop doing that during that period because all these nasty postings about this guy, as if somehow he was responsible for Mulder leaving the show. So tuned out of reality and hurtful.

[Doggett and Reyes] were hard to write for because your mindset is on Mulder and Scully for five, six years straight at that point. Then you've gotta write for two new people, and find new things about them.

Annabeth Gish's character, Reyes, was particularly hard to write for me, because she was a believer in tarot and spirituality and stuff like that. I don't believe in any of that stuff, so it was a little hard to write for her.

Monica Reyes made Mulder look mainstream by comparison.
Yeah, that was a little tricky. I never really got her voice down, but I liked the actress a lot; she's really talented.

How did you feel writing "Sunshine Days," knowing it was the last episode you'd do for *The X-Files*?

It was very bittersweet. It was not as fun to direct, as "Je Souhaite" was, and that was because I didn't do as good a job. I was so nervous that first time I directed on " Je Souhaite," that I was better prepared. The second time around, that *Brady Bunch* episode "Sunshine Days," I probably was not as prepared as I should have been. I made the crew work a little harder than they should have had to work because I was not as prepared. I was sorry about that.

It wasn't quite as much fun, partly because I knew this whole series was coming to an end. I was glad to get to say goodbye to the audience, as it were. There's a last scene in that episode where Scully talks about all the cases she's been on, and how she never got to the truth of what was behind all these paranormal things she had looked into, but at least she got to some kind of truth, which was that friends and love are important; that was something. She learned something from it all. It was a subtle way of saying goodbye to everybody, and it was nice to get to do that.

What did you do between the end of *The X-Files* and the beginning of *Breaking Bad*?

I spent an awful long time—four years—re-writing a script called *Tonight He Comes*, written by a talented writer named Vincent Ngo. I was hired by Michael Mann and Akiva Goldsman—the producers—to re-write it. They've named it *Hancock*, and it's coming out shortly. I spent a long time on what became *Hancock*.

What got me noticed by Michael Mann was that I wrote an episode of *Robbery Homicide Division*, which was a short-lived CBS show that Frank Spotnitz produced.[38] I wrote another episode, for Frank, of *Night Stalker*; that was a good show, and I'm sorry it didn't last longer.[39]

I've written a couple other movie scripts that have gone nowhere. I had a pilot for CBS with Mark Johnson called *Battle Creek*; that would have been a lot of fun, but CBS didn't want to do it. I went down the garden path with them for six months, and then they said, "No, we're not doing it."[40]

Frank and I had another pilot called *A.M.P.E.D.*, that would have been a Fox [produced] series, but they passed on it.[41] All of this is very much

---

[38] *Robbery Homicide Division* (2002–3) was created by Barry Schindel and broadcast by CBS. Gilligan wrote the fourth episode, "Free and Clear," which aired 18 October 2002.

[39] *Night Stalker* (2005) was developed by Frank Spotnitz, based on characters created by Jeff Rice and broadcast by ABC. The series—which starred Stuart Townsend as journalist Carl Kolchak—was an updated take on *Kolchak: The Night Stalker* (1974–5), the series that inspired Chris Carter to create *The X-Files*. Gilligan's episode, "What's the Frequency, Kolchak?" was the tenth and final episode produced. Though unaired by ABC, it was released on DVD with three other unscreened episodes and Darin Morgan's unproduced teleplay, "The M Word."

[40] After Gilligan's success with *Breaking Bad*, CBS revived *Battle Creek*. Because Gilligan was already committed to *Better Call Saul*, *House, M.D.* creator David Shore produced thirteen episodes which were broadcast in 2015. The series was not renewed for a second season.

[41] *A.M.P.E.D.* (2006) created by Frank Spotnitz & Vince Gilligan, concerned police officers—led by Detective Bryan Spicer (Lee Tergesen)—who must contend with a criminal element empowered by genetic mutations. A pilot was filmed for Spike TV,

par for the course, it's likely what's going on at any given moment in a working writer's career; stuff is on the back burner, and you're waiting for it to move to the front burner. It was a typical three or four years, where I was making a living getting stuff optioned, or writing stuff that wasn't being produced. It's nice now to actually have something that's going on the air. I'm trying to enjoy it while it lasts.

How did you conceive the idea for *Breaking Bad*?
I was talking to a buddy of mine, a writer friend named Tom Schnauz. He's a fellow NYU film grad I met twenty years ago. He is a talented writer, and I got him his start on *The Lone Gunmen*. He wrote for us on that show, and then he wrote for *The X-Files*. Now he's a successful writer on the tv show *Reaper*.[42] He's one of their go-to guys on that show.

I was talking to him one day about three years ago, and we were bemoaning the business—how hard it is to get a pilot going, how hard it is to get a script sold and produced—just pissing and moaning about everything under the sun. What else could we do, because writing sucks? The writing itself is great, but all the professional aspects of it stink.

---

but the series was not greenlit.

[42] After *Reaper* was cancelled in 2008, Schnauz joined Gilligan on *Breaking Bad*'s third season. He remained with the series through its conclusion, briefly worked on *Resurrection* in 2014, then rejoined Gilligan for the *Breaking Bad* spinoff, *Better Call Saul*, in 2015.

What are we gonna do next? How about being a greeter at Walmart? That looks like a job you don't have to take home with you every night. What about selling crystal meth out of the back of an RV, traveling the country?

That kind of hit me—not as a potential career move—this idea of the character that became Walter White (Bryan Cranston) popped into my head at that point, this guy who is not a criminal, but is involved in criminal activities. He's very much a straight arrow, and yet he's "breaking bad," which is an old Southern expression that means to raise hell. He's this otherwise good man, so what reason would he be doing that? It quickly came that he has nothing to lose; he's dying of cancer, and he's trying to provide for his family.

[Ideas] usually don't come together that quickly, but this character just launched himself into my head. I got very excited about it, partly because it came together so quickly; usually, it's much more laborious than that. I had the luck of my ignorance, because I came up with this character who cooks crystal meth to save his family and is dying. I thought, I've got as good a chance of getting this made as anything.

It's ridiculous on the face of it! Everyone should say no to that, and I'm astounded to this day that someone said yes. I can't get over it. Someone in Hollywood, circa 2006, said yes to this! The film and tv business is so cautious—in so many ways—especially the movie business. Basic cable's having something of a renaissance, but broadcast networks and movies are playing it pretty safe.

They're all part of conglomerates that provide your internet service; all of these creative issues are subject to the whims of bean counters, and their actuarial tables, cost sheets, and whatever the hell else I'm trying to say. None of this stuff makes any sense to me; it's all gibberish.

It's not about people getting excited by a story anymore, and taking a flyer on their enthusiasm and their passion. In the midst of all that, getting this show off the ground—frankly, I don't know how it happened, but I'm enormously grateful that AMC came along and took a chance.

Did you target basic cable with *Breaking Bad*, or was it pitched to the networks first?
I'd had a deal with Sony Television. They'd been very good to me a few years before, when Mark Johnson and I pitched *Battle Creek* to CBS. Sony was the studio, and really liked the pilot script. It was a story about a cash-poor police department in Battle Creek, Michigan. They've got no money for wiretaps, or proper investigative equipment; they need more tax payers in their town.

Across from their office opens an FBI field office, and now they've got a stunningly good-looking FBI agent with all this money at his disposal. "You need a helicopter with an infrared camera? How many do you want? I'll get you three of 'em." He has this infrastructure at his fingertips, and all the women—including the one our hero is pining for—are in love with this guy. On top of everything else, he's a great guy; you can't even hate him.

In the pilot, they find a body and the [FBI agent] becomes the lead investigator by virtue of having answered the phone. It turns out to be Jimmy Hoffa that they've found. It would have been a fun series.

All the executives at CBS liked it, except [President and CEO] Les Moonves. He's the only one you need to like it!

I didn't mean to get off on this tangent, but my point was that Sony liked working with me on this pilot. Once Moonves shot us down, that was it for that, because he's not going to let us take it somewhere else. Sony left it with, "We'd like to work with you again someday, so if you ever have an idea for us, we'll make a pilot commitment, if it's an idea we like."

So I had this idea, and said, "What the hell?" I went and pitched them the idea for *Breaking Bad*, and Zack Van Amburg and Jamie Erlicht—the two co-heads of production over there at Sony TV—sat there and listened to me pitch this thing for half an hour, stone-faced. I liked these guys. This was a worthy effort, but there's no way they can do a show about a guy selling crystal meth, and then they looked at each other and said, "We'll get back to you." I'm thinking that's it for that.

Three or four days later, they called and said, "We're going to buy it." Then it was a matter of finding a network, and these Sony guys were behind it from the start. They went with we me as I pitched it to TNT, who were very pleasant about it: "We like the story, we just can't put a show on the air about a guy cooking crystal meth. We'll all be fired." They passed.

I pitched it to HBO, which was the opposite experience. The lady at HBO, who's no longer there, I pitched it to her with flop sweat dripping down my head, for twenty minutes straight. She was counting the tiles on the ceiling. Never got back to us after the pitch about whether she liked it or not, but I assumed that was a no.

Finally, we wound up at FX, and they bought it. I wrote the pilot for them, and they owned it. They're a good bunch at FX, smart people. I left there liking and respecting them very much. Any small cable outlet only has a finite amount of production that they can do, and they can't do everything. They thought long and hard about it and wanted to do it, but they passed on it.

I thought it was dead in the water at that point, because it had to be cable or nothing; there's no way in hell a network's going to put that on the air.

A then-junior agent—who's career has since gone very nicely—a guy named Mark Gordon[43] who's at ICM now, took the liberty of sending the pilot script to friends of his at AMC, two executives there, Ben Davis and Jeremy Elice. Mark sent this to them, then called me up and said the folks at AMC were interested.

I said, "AMC? They show old movies!" This was before *Mad Men*.

---

[43] As of November 2015, Gordon was the head of International Scripted Television for ICM. He's not to be confused with the producer of the same name, famous for *Grey's Anatomy*, among many others.

He said, "They're interested. Why don't you meet with them?"

I though, if I meet with them, we'll meet in a bar and I'll get a free scotch out of it. I met with Christina Wayne, the big wig there on the creative end, and Ben and Jeremy. They said to me, "We'd really like to do this show on our network."

I said, "Okay, great," not believing a word of it. Lo and behold, they were serious, and they found a way not only to produce the show, but they had to buy it from FX, which took a number of months. I really appreciate FX, they were good guys, that they would allow it.

It's the worst thing you can do, as a company, to develop something and then shove it in a drawer, and never allow minds behind it to sell it to somebody else. It's a terrible thing that's endemic in this business. That's the way it worked with *Battle Creek* at CBS. Les Moonves is never going to let a script go to another network, or another company; he's never going to let that happen. I understand the business side of it, but karma-wise, it's not too cool.

If you don't want to do the show, let somebody pay you the money back and take a whack at it. Then it's no harm, no foul, if it becomes a hit elsewhere. It shouldn't reflect badly on you; it's not like you made the wrong decision.

FX were mensches about it, and they let the script go. God bless them for it, and I'll always remember that. AMC produced it and here we are. I can't believe we're here, and I'm very grateful.

How much research about crystal meth did you have to do?
A fair bit. I read several books on the subject, both from the point of view of the DEA and from the point of view of the addicts. Fortunately or unfortunately—depending on how you look at it—all this stuff's readily available. Internet searches will tell you how to make the stuff, what the formula is, as well as all the better uses of that information technology—where you can get help as an addict.

Frank Spotnitz's brother-in-law, Grant, is a DEA agent, and he was very helpful to me. I got to have lunch with him and his partner when they were stationed in Riverside, California. I asked some questions about what it's like from the DEA point of view. The DEA has been wonderfully supportive of our efforts, in showing how they work.

We have a character on our show who is a DEA agent. He's colorful, he's a bit of a cowboy, but he is a very good cop. He cares about what he does for a living and knows that it's important. We try to portray him in a well-rounded fashion, and try to show the DEA as realistically as we can, which is an organization of people who really believe in what they're doing and who work very hard. They've been very helpful in making certain elements of the show realistic.

I knew nothing about crystal meth before all of this started. I just knew it was really bad for you. All the research I've done has not changed that opinion one bit; it's a terrible drug and in no way, shape, or form do we try to make it look any more than it is. It's bad for you, it tears apart whole communities.

That's not even the point of the show, for me. The point of the show is about a guy who's having the world's worst mid-life crisis, and who does something terrible in order to do something good. Then the question arises, do the ends justify the means? I think we're not-so-gradually making the point that no, the ends don't justify the means.

Do you hold back some of the science so the audience doesn't gain too much knowledge of dangerous chemistry from the show?
Absolutely. Thermite, in particular. Thermite couldn't be much easier to make. It's basically two ingredients. We only really talked about one of them. We want the audience to know that the science exists, and the science itself is fascinating, but we're not a primer for how to make crystal meth, thermite, or fulminated mercury. That's not what we're about.

MacGyver was a fun show, and we're borrowing a little bit from that in the sense that Walt is a teacher and a chemistry whiz, and I like that post-modern *MacGyver* aspect we occasionally touch on, where he puts together a bomb or who knows what? We've got all kinds of crazy stuff he's doing in season two.

How did you write my favorite line: Jesse Pinkman's character-defining dialogue about "the cow house…where they live?"
I'm so tickled that you say that. People on the set still quote that one, and that's the best feeling for a writer, when people quote a line back to you. I think of all the movies that I love, and certain phrases just enter the vernacular, like "Make my day," from Clint Eastwood in *Dirty Harry*.

It made me chuckle when I wrote it, because I knew the character was kind of a numbnuts. That's how I saw him at the time, but Jesse is growing on me; he's not quite the dope that I first thought he was. He's revealing himself to be something more than that, but at the time [of the pilot], I saw him as just a knucklehead.

It was not the line that you love until the actor read it. Aaron Paul's line reading was so funny that everyone on the set that day had to bite the inside of their mouths to keep from laughing. As soon as I called cut, they all started laughing. It was only then that I knew it was a good line, and people still quote it back to me.

[The line] only partially exists on the page, then the right actor reads it and it reaches its true potential as a quotable line.

Given that *Breaking Bad* must occur within Walt's remaining lifetime of approximately two years, do you think shows like *24* and *Lost* have made smaller narrative windows more appealing?
I think so, particularly *24*, because everyone understands the clock. When it first went on the air I thought, that's a great idea. Then I thought, I'm glad I'm not on that writing staff! As fun as it sounds, that would be miserable to plot every week, but they do a great job on that show.

I guess that applies to *Lost* too, but I'm not a regular viewer. I confess I didn't realize it took place in a finite amount of time. Someone told me later that they'd only been on the island for forty days, or something. It'd been four years, and I was like, "What?"

The difference between *24* and *Lost* is that I explicitly understand the clock, but I didn't glean [the short time scale] from *Lost*. With *Lost*, I don't think it matters that they've only been there forty days.

What was behind the decision to put the language in *Breaking Bad* that has to be muted when it airs on AMC?
This is still an ongoing argument. [AMC] really doesn't want me doing words that they have to mute. I don't want to go backward. To me, the horse is kind of out of the barn now. We've got characters on our show who are never going to say "freakin'." They're never going to tone down their language.

The audience gets it; the audience does the math. I know some people were expressing their disappointment in the words being dropped out, but to me, the alternative is less palatable, which is to change the way people talk. I'd rather have them talk the way they would talk. Having said that, even last season, we'd have the occasional F-word, but we'd only have two per hour that we would then have to bleep. It's not like we had a string of them.

There are very byzantine rules that seem to change week to week. They don't seem hard and fast; they seem kind of arbitrary.

I watch a show Saturday nights on Fox—*Mad TV*—and they bleep the F-word all the time. I prefer bleeping, because then you know you're missing something. I think we made a mistake first season to dip [the audio], but that was AMC's call. I wrote it for bleeping.

I think the audience gets it, they do the math in their head, and it feels more authentic that way. You're not having the actual word, but everyone knows what the word is, and then you have value added when you get to the DVD set; you can sell the DVD uncut or unbleeped. That's my argument.

There's no perfect scenario there, because we're never going to be allowed to be HBO and have every F-word [audible]. The least egregious way to go about it—the smallest sin—would be to have them talk the way they really would talk, and then just bleep the objectionable words. I'm hoping to win that battle, but we'll see. I may not.[44]

What do you look for in hiring writers for *Breaking Bad*?
I look for good visual storytelling. We take pride in our dialogue, but this is visual storytelling. It's the difference between a play and a screenplay. A stage play is all about the dialogue, and I've seen and read some wonderful ones, but that's not what we're doing here. We're telling a story through the images.

I specifically look for visual writing, which is to say not the dialogue on the page, but the action lines, the scene description. How much is the writer getting across through a look—through a bit of body language, the omission of an action or the action itself—versus a writer who gets everything across verbally.

---

[44] Both *Breaking Bad* and its spinoff, *Better Call Saul*, continue to feature language beyond that which AMC will broadcast. As Vince predicted, the uncensored nature of the DVDs and Blu-rays became a selling point.

In real life, very often, we don't always say what we mean; very often we say the opposite, or we don't say anything at all.

How did the strike affect your plans for *Breaking Bad*?
We had two more episodes we were going to do. We had an order for eight, and we only got through six because of the strike.

I'm very sorry the strike had to happen. It was a shame for a lot of reasons, but a bit of a silver lining for us, oddly enough, is that we didn't get to do our last two episodes [for season one]. We had plotted out all our episodes before the show ever went on the air, and we didn't know how well the show would be received.

Not knowing how the public would take to it, you tend—at least I do—to want to be a little more sensational. You want to really keep the show exciting and interesting and keep 'em watching. Those last two episodes—because of that—would have been really big episodes, and they would have taken the characters into a hugely different realm than that they were already in; it would have been a hard thing to come back from, coming into season two.[45]

We're not just picking up and doing those two episodes at the start of this season, [season two]. We threw those out completely, and we're starting somewhere else. We're building more slowly than we would have otherwise built. I think that's really good, because I know we've all

---

[45] As Gilligan revealed in numerous *Breaking Bad* interviews over the succeeding seasons, he'd planned to kill off Jesse Pinkman (Aaron Paul) in the first season finale.

had our favorite shows that were really interesting up to a certain point, but maybe they go too far, and then there's no going back from it.

To me, the trick is to do as little as you can with the characters, and yet keep them as interesting as possible. It's a real balancing act. You don't want to be incredibly dramatic week in, week out; you want to bury it. We start off season two with a couple of really dramatically big episodes, then we want to throttle back a little and quiet things down, modulate it, have some quieter, more character-based episodes, and then the bigger, plottier episodes. Mix 'em up; that's what keeps a show interesting.

When will season two of *Breaking Bad* air?
January of 2009. I kind of wish we were going on the air sooner than that. Having said that, we have an awful lot of work between now and then, so it's good to have that amount of time. I'm hoping people don't forget about us.

What's your proudest accomplishment as a writer?
Breaking Bad. It's the first show I've run myself. It's my baby, and as much as I loved *The X-Files*, it was Chris Carter's baby, and I was a very well-treated employee there. The best job I ever had was *The X-Files*, where I didn't have all the responsibility and could have that much more fun writing individual episodes, learning to be a producer, and learning to direct. That was more sheer fun than this is.

[*Breaking Bad*] is more responsibility than fun, but this is what I'm proudest of, getting to create something fully. Not to say it's not a group effort, we have wonderful writers, a wonderful cast, and wonderful crew people; this is very much a group effort. The fact that I got to come up with the idea in the first place is very thrilling, and I'm very proud of that.

JOHN SHIBAN
19 June 2008

How did you become interested in screenwriting?
When I was very young—in junior high, high school—I was very much into science fiction and fantasy. I wanted to be a short story writer. I wanted to be Harlan Ellison, Ray Bradbury, or someone like that; that was my dream. When I got to college, I kind of got the movie bug, started attending film classes at UCLA, started seeing a lot of movies I hadn't seen before, outside genre work. I said to myself, "I want to make movies." It was at that time that I shifted over from English major to film student, and I was on my way.

How did you come to the attention of Chris Carter?
It was a combination of "It's all who you know" and a bit of luck and being ready when you get the call.

After UCLA, I went to the AFI[46] graduate program in screenwriting. Among the people I met there was Frank Spotnitz. We became friends, and kept in touch after graduating. We'd send each other our scripts and give notes, and try to network, etc. He got hooked up with Chris and got his staff job in the middle of season two.

I had been writing feature scripts and hadn't thought about tv much; I thought I was going to write features, a whole different animal. I'd probably still be writing spec features to this day, it's such a crazy business.

I was writing these feature scripts and sending them to Frank, and he would give notes. I had an agent, and was trying to get things set up, etc. I had a day job in computers—in programming, systems testing in Camarillo—so I was commuting from my apartment in Westwood to Camarillo every day and writing at night, that life that everybody has done once in their lives.

One day late in the spring I get this phone call from Frank and he said, "What are you doing?" and I said, "Well, I'm at work," and he said, "Well it's the last day of the season. Chris is going on hiatus tomorrow and he said to me that he's kind of tired of all the old-school tv writers who come in with their own way of doing things. He'd like to hire a staff writer who has no tv experience, so he can show him the way that Chris Carter does it." Frank said, "I told him about you, showed him

---

[46] The American Film Institute, founded in 1965 by presidential mandate, has—since 1969—operated the AFI conservatory, an accredited graduate school that offers degrees in six disciplines, including screenwriting.

one of your scripts, and he wants to meet you, but you've got to come in today."

I go to my boss and I literally said to him, "Oh, I have this stomach ache. I don't feel good," and I hopped into my Pinto station wagon. I drive from Camarillo to Fox, find his office, and I had a very nice meeting with Chris.

I knew the show, and I'd seen some of it and I liked it, but I wasn't like a hard-core fan at the time. I knew who Chris was, but I didn't know his whole back story and whatnot. We're chatting away and he said, "What inspires you? How did you get to this point?" I said, "One of the reasons why I think I would be good for your show is that one of my favorite shows growing up was *The Night Stalker*," and he said, "Oh, really? Me too." I was like, "Yeah, isn't that cool." We were just chatting about *The Night Stalker*, and so we had this nice meeting.

Then I go back to work, and the next day was the longest day of my life. I knew he was leaving and I knew he had to make the decision and I didn't hear anything. This was May of 1995, so I didn't have a cell phone; you called your house phone—your answering machine—every fifteen minutes to see if somebody called. I was just about to leave and get into the car to go home when I check again, and there was a call from Fox Business Affairs.

I called them back, and they said, "We want to offer you a staff job."

I said, "Okay."

The next week I was there, so it was an overnight success that took years and years.

What was it like walking into *The X-Files* offices for the first time as a staff writer?

It was thrilling and terrifying at the same time. I was so inexperienced on what a working writer's life was like—what a [writers'] room was like, and what a staff position was like—that it probably saved me from just running away and breaking down in tears. It's a big deal, and I didn't realize how big a deal it was until I got there. Holy shit. This is not what everybody else gets to do. It was a special place, in good ways and bad. It wasn't easy, but I was thrilled.

The great thing about Chris was he didn't really care much about titles and whatnot. He just wanted good, smart people around him that he could bounce off. The first week I was in the room helping them break the season three opener, "The Blessing Way" and "Paper Clip." Two weeks ago I was doing postal software testing in Camarillo. Now I'm sitting here with Chris Carter, helping him break this big two-parter. It was awesome.

How did you conceive your first story, the paraplegic murder mystery, "The Walk?"

I came in with a bunch of ideas. Each of the writers came in to Chris—and Howard [Gordon] was there, Frank was there—and would throw out ideas. I had to do the crash course from the time I got the job. I got my hands on as many VHS tapes as I could, and caught up on episodes.

I pitched a couple ideas that ended up being later episodes, including my first one, which was "The Walk." While I was watching a bunch of these *X-Files* late at night, I turned off the VCR and this old Marlon Brando movie called *The Man* was on, which is about a World War II vet who is paralyzed from the waist down; it's a '50s social drama about adapting to things post-war. Because of my science fiction and fantasy background, I had read about astral projection. It just popped into my head—that would be cool—and that was one of the first three or four ideas I pitched. Chris and Howard looked at each other and said, "That sounds like an episode. Work on that one."

They didn't always come that easy.

How did you adapt to Ten Thirteen's boarding procedure?
I really responded to it; it made sense to me. I'm doing it right now. I'm looking at a board for another project as we speak. The reason why I ended up in a software day job was because of the way my brain works. The logic to it and the rigorousness of it clicked with me. It's fair to say that over the years, Frank and I would end up breaking—with the writers—80% of the stories. I have an affinity for the structure.

When I was writing features, I would take movies that I liked and break them down onto cards, to find out how they structured the damned thing so that I could structure my own.

How did the frequent writing partnership of Gilligan-Shiban-Spotnitz develop?
We became friends, and we all had a similar sense of humor and similar

taste. When Vince came on halfway through [season] three, I was there to help him learn how we do the boards. We clicked and started doing boards together.

We had a script ["Leonard Betts"] from an outside writer that came in, and the draft was just not there—this was probably season four, or late three—and Chris asked Frank to divide it up between him and me and Vince to rewrite this thing in a short period of time. That was the first time we did it, and we liked doing it that way; so it became something that we weren't doing just to fix people's [scripts]. "Monday," for example, we broke together and pounded [the script] out. It was a way to get the job done, and we all trusted each other and knew our strengths. It made a good collaboration.

How did you conceive "S.R. 819," which reinvigorated FBI Assistant Director Walter Skinner (Mitch Pileggi)?
I had an image in my head, that I pitched to Frank and Chris, of Skinner in a boxing ring. It just felt right to me. Sometimes, as a writer, when you get those feelings, you go with them. I had the same feeling with "Elegy," where I said "haunted bowling alley." It just feels right, I can't explain why. Skinner in the boxing ring, in a way, made his character a little more interesting.

In addition to science fiction and fantasy, I was always a big John le Carre and film noir fan. I pulled some of the noirish elements that I loved from *D.O.A.* and *Out of the Past* and *The Killers* and made a Skinner story.

The interesting thing about the *D.O.A.* part of it—and Chris suggested this—in the original pitch, Skinner in the boxing ring was one thing over here, but the main story was going to be how Skinner helps Mulder, who has the [multiplying carbon] in him. Chris said, "Here's an idea"—and I remember this because it was really insightful, and I've used it ever since—"the audience knows we're not going to kill David Duchovny's character, but we might kill Mitch's character." That really gave a whole other element to it. It added a tension that made Mulder and Scully's part better.

Who was Arthur Dales, and how did he become immortalized in "Travelers" as Mulder's X-File-investigating predecessor?
Our screenwriting teacher, that Frank and I both had [at AFI], was an amazing man named Howard Dimsdale. He had been blacklisted during the McCarthy era, went to England for a while, but came back here and kept working. One of his pseudonyms was Arthur Dales; you'll see his name popping up here and there on all kinds of things. He was really an inspiration to me and to Frank; I think we were both looking for a nod to him, because he had passed away soon after we graduated. We were looking for a way to give a nod to this guy.

The nice thing about "Travelers" was that it was a way not only to name a character after him, but to deal with some of the issues that he dealt with in his life, namely the blacklist, communist scares, etc. How do you tie that to *The X-Files*? Well, maybe that's the origin of the x-files. I don't know if it was a fan favorite—because of the lack of Mulder and Scully—but I've always liked that one because it's about history, about America. It was a lot of fun to build that animal.

How did writing for the Lone Gunmen differ from doing the traditional X-File?

There were comedy episodes [in *The X-Files*]; Darin Morgan, obviously, did some brilliant work, with offbeat humor, but the Gunmen could really be comedic characters, and that was very refreshing. You could have an X-File that was a romp and still scary. It's not tongue in cheek, it's very sincere, but it was really refreshing and fun to be able to do a scene that was slapstick. We eventually did do that with Mulder and Scully, in "Dreamland," with Michael McKean.

It was an interesting process to see how malleable the show was. I wasn't there when "Humbug" was done [in season two], but I know there was a lot of anxiety—are we killing the series, is it going to survive this episode? It did. For the X-Files world to still make sense proved that, if the audience loves your characters, they'll go a lot further than you would ever imagine.

Season eight's "Badlaa" eclipses even Chris Carter's sewer extravaganza "The Host" as the most disgusting concept in the show's history. How did you conceive that story?

Giving credit where credit is due, I came in with a pitch about this guy with no legs on the cart—the Indian mystic—who uses his powers against people. One of the powers in my pitch was that he can manipulate his own body size and squeeze into something. I had this scene I pitched to Chris where he takes his hand and starts to push it into this guy's ear. He's squirming in horror as this guy climbs inside his head.

Chris said, "Why his head? Why not his ass? That's scarier to me!"

I said, "You're damn right!"

And so, the butt genie, as we started calling him, was born that day. It was so outlandish. "You think can we get away with that?" We did.

Any comments from Fox Broadcast Standards and Practices on that episode?
"We give up."

How did directing "Underneath" change you as a writer?
It gave me a renewed respect for how hard it was to produce the damn thing. Decades hence, when they wonder why *The X-Files* mattered to television, one of the things the show did was elevate the level of storytelling and filmmaking on television. There are other shows that have done that too, but *The X-Files* was certainly one of the shows that tried to make movie-quality work every week. When you have to sit down and look at those callsheets, get those shots, have the sets be right and up to that standard, it's really hard. I have a lot of respect for the Kim Manners, Rob Bowmans, and David Nutters[47] of the world who contributed to that level of quality.

It was very educational to see some of the things that you would sweat over [as a writer] that didn't matter and other things that you hadn't sweated over mattered greatly.

---

[47] Kim Manners, Rob Bowman, and David Nutter were—in descending order—the three most prolific directors to helm episodes of *The X-Files*. Manners (1951–2009) was reunited with Shiban on *Supernatural*.

I've done some directing since then; I did a horror movie called *Rest Stop*,[48] but I think my writing has definitely changed. I find myself fretting more over blocking than I ever did—where are you going to put these people when they're having this conversation? Somebody has to [block those scenes]. It makes a better script—even if it's not written completely to camera—there are ways to imply camera position by just the way you write and how little you say, and what you show or don't show. All of that is really important, especially in this genre.

If you're trying to be scary, you have to control what the audience sees and when they see it, so the script needs to do that, too. That's the first place to do it.

With David Amann, you plotted "Release," which wrapped up the story of John Doggett's son; was that something you felt had to be handled before the series ended?
I loved working with Robert [Patrick], we all did. Doggett sort of had a thankless role, to a certain extent; he had to fill Mulder's shoes, and then Mulder came back. We all felt the character should get a big sendoff.

Not by coincidence, all of us had either just had their first child or were about to. We were all at that age when we were having kids, and that's such a potent bit of character backstory that we felt we wanted to explore. I was really pleased with how that came out.

---

[48] *Rest Stop: Dead Ahead* (2006) was written and directed by John Shiban. It was the first release in Warner Studio's direct-to-DVD horror imprint, Raw Feed.

Are there any stories you wanted to do, but never worked out?
There was one I said in a room on another show...what was it? We did the backwards-told episode. We did a lot of stuff.

You know, we never did the *Some Like It Hot* episode; we never did Mulder in drag, and it's probably a good thing that we never did. I remember we talked about it once or twice...

I've seen Duchovny in drag.
Yeah, that's right! We probably should have done it.

You could have had a nice *Twin Peaks* crossover.[49]
Yeah!

How did *The X-Files* prepare you for writing *Supernatural*?
In two big ways: this kind of horror procedural, it carries with it a lot of potential dangers. That's why a lot of the attempts to do this kind of show since *The X-Files* have failed, not only in controlling the standalones, but in building an overarching mythology, not that we always successfully avoided confusion. The fans of this kind of show want that, they want both a thrill this week and a big story for the characters to be involved in. From my first meeting with [*Supernatural* creator] Eric Kripke, it was "I need your help in figuring this damned thing out."

---

[49] David Duchovny played Dennis (aka Denise) Bryson, a transvestite DEA agent, in three second-season episodes of *Twin Peaks*. With *Twin Peaks* set to follow *The X-Files* back to television in 2017, Duchovny told *TV Line*, "Yeah, I'll shave my legs," in reference to reprising the role of Agent Bryson.

The other thing is the boarding process, and that's applied to all the jobs I've had since *X-Files*, learning how to break stories that way. Having the opportunity and the chance to do it for 220 episodes—or whatever it was—is the ultimate film school. That has served me in features and in television and in everything, because that's where it starts: the story. That what I brought to *Supernatural*, and that's what I'm going to bring to whatever I do next.

What's next for you?
I've just finished a sequel to this *Rest Stop* movie—*Rest Stop: Don't Look Back*. We shot that back in the fall, and we just delivered it to Warner Brothers.[50]

I'm moving on to a couple television projects that I'm trying to get set up. I'd like to direct another feature, and so I have a project with a producer that we're about to go out with. I'm spinning a lot of plates right now, after surviving the strike.

---

[50] Shiban wrote but did not direct *Rest Stop: Don't Look Back* (2008), the fifth release from Raw Feed.

HOWARD GORDON
24 June 2008

How did you become interested in screenwriting?
I have always been, almost to the exclusion of anything else, a television fan. I never came out [to Los Angeles] aspiring to be a movie writer; I loved television and the idea of writing for it. It was something I always thought I would do, from an early age.

I briefly, during college, flirted with being a poet and a short story writer, but reverted to my older fantasy of becoming a television writer. I brought some of my high-minded ideals when I moved out here after college, pimping a screenplay about Lord Byron; it was a miniseries that my partner and I had concocted. No one was interested in the Lord Byron screenplay, so we had to settle for the *St. Elsewhere* spec script that we had written.

My partner is Alex Gansa.

How did the two of you met?
We met at Princeton, in our senior year, over our mutual love of Saul Bellow. Both of us were going to get our masters in fine arts in fiction and creative writing. We decided to try our luck out in Hollywood, knowing no one, piled into my Datsun D210, and went across country.

[We] started an SAT preparation course for the affluent, private school crowd. It was a very peer-to-peer idea, where recent graduates from Ivy League colleges would teach your kids; that was the premise. Most of [the teachers] were aspiring writers themselves; a lot of them went on to become writers for *Simpsons*, *King of the Hill*, and *Saturday Night Live*. My teachers included Greg Daniels [co-creator of *King of the Hill*, developer of the US version of *The Office*], Jonathan Mostow [director of *Terminator 3: Rise of the Machines*], Alek Keshishian [writer-director of *Love and Other Disasters*], and a bunch of people who've gone on to great success in the tv and movie business.

How did you and Alex land jobs at *The X-Files*?
Alex and I had been on *Beauty and the Beast* (1987–90) at Witt/Thomas [Productions]. After *Beauty and the Beast*, we wrote a pilot called *Country Estates* [in 1993] about a cul-du-sac where there's a black family and a white family; it was kind of heightened reality, but it was something that was shot.

Chris Carter had pitched [another series] to ABC, and they said we're doing a similar idea. He read [*Country Estates*] and liked it, so we were on Chris's radar when he then came up with one of his next ideas, which was *X-Files*, and he hired us.

How would you describe the atmosphere, early on, at *The X-Files*?
It was really wonderful. We took the job over the advice of our agent, who said, "Why do you want to be on a Friday night show?" Fox was this tenuous network; this was a tenuous show on a tenuous network, and our agent said, "It's a Friday night show about aliens. What good could come of it?" On top of that [*The X-Files*] wasn't even the hot show on Fox, which was [*The Adventures of Brisco County, Jr.*].

We saw [*The X-Files* pilot] and completely fell in love, thought it was one of the best things we'd seen. The pilot really is one of the best that has ever been done because the DNA for the series was all contained in it. The promise of what it would become was right there.

What was really special about that [first] year was that the people who were there: Glen Morgan and Jim Wong, Alex and me, and Chris. There was this tremendous camaraderie and competition, in all the best ways, and low expectations [from the network]. It was a Friday night show, which didn't have many expectations attached to it. We got the chance to do what we wanted. We all learned from each other a lot and got to create something very special.

Was the Ten Thirteen boarding process new to you?
We had done versions of it. Glen and Jim perfected it. It was a way to think, very rigorously, about the story process. If you could put a verb and a noun—a simple sentence—about somebody does something, it gave you the pit of the scene. It forced you to think about it in that concise way. That was the kind of storytelling we did on *X-Files*.

How did you and Alex work as a team?

I'll write this scene, you'll write that scene, and we'll put it together and see if it's working. Or, I'll write this act and you'll write that act. The more familiar we got with each other—and the more contempt developed between us—we wound up trying to avoid each other, stay out of each other's way. We started writing more alone, separately. We never wrote in a room together; that was never what we did. We would often rewrite each other's stuff, so I'd say, "Let me take a crack at this," or I'd give him very very big notes, or he'd give me big notes, that kind of thing. It was a very very fluid process, but it was never done over a typewriter or a computer simultaneously.

Was backstory established in shows like "Conduit" and "Lazarus" narrative real estate that writers were eager to claim?

When you have a new show, everything's kind of a tabula rasa. The pilot is the suggestion of where the show might go. It's a kind of gold rush for backstory. Does Mulder have a father or mother? All those characters—all that life—has not yet been explored. That happens in the first couple of years in the show, and you wind up fishing out that pond and it gets harder and harder.

How did writing without Alex differ when your partnership split in season two?

It was profound. I can't underestimate the panic I felt, because when you write so closely with somebody, you really do become this entity. Your creative process is defined by that, and you externalize, in many ways, so many aspects of the process. I had to internalize and take care of myself, and it created quite a bit of anxiety for me, frankly.

Given that "Sleepless" arose from your insomnia, where did you look for stories?
All of the obvious places. If you look at *X-Files* in those first few years, all the obvious mythologies were exploited, whether it's ghosts, vampires, possessions, reincarnation; those are pretty obvious horror tropes that we exploited. Once those became spoken for—and you could maybe repeat it once or twice—you have to really, really dig hard for things.

I always told myself that when I wrote an episode about time travel or invisibility, I'd told my last two stories. That's roughly what happened in season four. If I ever stooped that low, I've run out of ideas and shouldn't be on the show anymore.

The ideas try to come from a place of metaphor, and how does this [metaphor] interact with the character? Max (Scott Bellis) is interesting in "Fallen Angel" because he's kind of a nut, nobody listens to him, and he was an accelerated or distorted version of Mulder himself—the chicken little. Nobody listened to him. He was an unreliable witness, but he was also carrying the truth with him. That's an intriguing character to explore.

The character in "D.P.O.," Darin Oswald, [is] this idiot slacker kid who suddenly has all this power. The most interesting part is always when the supernatural interacts with the character. That was always my approach to story: what's a character I am interested in seeing here?

How did you come to write the Skinner-centric episode "Avatar?"
It was David Duchovny's idea. [Skinner's] one of those underexploited characters. I don't really know anything about him. Let me tell a story about him. It's that simple.

[The episode] came also at a time when I was working so hard my own marriage was being challenged by the workload. That became part of the substance of Skinner's challenge: what's the price of this work we do? It's a theme I've carried into *24*.

"Grotesque" is one of the few *X-Files* that could be interpreted as lacking a supernatural element.
That's an interesting one, because almost to a fault, the great thing about *X-Files* is that the unreal part is always more interesting. It is more interesting that it's aliens and not just a heat variation; the scientific explanation's always less interesting than the supernatural one, which is why *X-Files* worked. It was about a paranoid guy who happened to be right about his version of the world.

In the case of "Grotesque," I did a draft and it *was* one of those [supernatural] things that fought back. I tried to find a supernatural aspect to this, and it just wasn't working. In the end, it was the power of Agent Patterson's (Kurtwood Smith) distorted mind that made the story make sense for me, and made it writable.

There was a whole [supernatural] draft that I threw out; I don't even remember anymore, but it involved gargoyles and grotesques that actually existed.

The original draft was a more traditional *X-Files* story.
It was, and it didn't work. [The produced version] allowed a much darker psychological interpretation of events.

It also allowed Mulder's view—the most outré explanation—to be wrong for once.
Right. In this case, too, the best stories tended to be something in which Mulder saw something of himself in them. This was a mentor who was in some ways taking Mulder through the paces that might lie ahead for him if he's not careful, and if he chases monsters.

What was the hardest part of running the writers' room?
It was an enjoyable process in its own masochistic way. It's great when you finally figure it out, that's probably the way to describe it. It feels hopeless for so long and for so many days—sometimes days on end—and then, suddenly, something happens that makes it all fall into place. That continues to be the satisfaction with the writing process.

It's a fairly miserable process to me. There are moments of real dread attached to it—when you really think I cannot figure this out, there is no solution—and then, suddenly or incrementally, the solution finds itself; it's not always a great or elegant solution, but it's a workable one and it's one that keeps episode seven from bumping into episode nine.

Were there any stories that you never figured out how to execute?
Yeah, there is one that I threw out, and it became "Sleepless." It involved sort of Frankenstein genetic engineering experiment that had gone wrong in this farming community. I bit off more than I could

chew with that idea and never quite solved it. In some ways, I took that material and used it in *Strange World*, which was the series I did after *X-Files*.

With "Unrequited" (invisibility) and "Synchrony" (time travel), were you officially out of ideas in season four?
I just couldn't contribute any more. I really played my last hand. I gave to the show all I was ever going to give it, and I got from it all I was ever going to get from it. I was younger and probably more restless then than I am now; I would have told you then no one should ever be on a show for more than four years. Here I am in the seventh year of *24*, but I would have sworn up and down.

At the time, except for Chris, I was the only one who'd been on the show from the beginning. Glen and Jim had left by the second year, and had come and gone a number of times. Alex left after the first year. Frank [Spotnitz] didn't come on until the end of the second, and so I had been there longer than anyone but Chris. I thought the show maybe has a year or two left in it…little did I know.

When you first heard the concept of *24*, what was your initial reaction to the real-time element?
I saw this pilot and it was the best thing I've seen since *X-Files*.

With *X-Files*, I always felt it was a championship basketball team and I was the fifth guy on the floor. I was so impressed with Chris, but also with Glen and Jim, with Darin Morgan and, frankly, with Vince. I got to work with some brilliant people, and I always felt like the journeyman among them. I was pleased with some of the episodes. Occasionally, some were quite good, but these guys were doing one great show after the next, almost without fail.

I had a second-class citizen status [on *The X-Files*], yet on *24*—right from the beginning—I connected, felt real ownership in the show, and real authorship. Bob [Cochran] and Joel [Surnow] created this show that was, first of all, revolutionary in the storytelling, but it was a way of telling stories that really was comfortable for me; I took to it very easily, very intuitively.

What were the initial challenges in writing real-time teleplays?
Because it really came to me naturally, the challenges were always trusting the illusion of real time; even an otherwise mundane scene was somehow more interesting because we were in this amazing narrative experiment of real time.

In some ways, it was a process. I thought this about *X-Files*, too. How many times can there be an alien encounter and Scully just misses it by happening to be in the wrong place? How many times can she be looking away, and how many times can there be an alien thing? Then Glen and Jim—in the third episode—[create] Tooms [in "Squeeze"]. Suddenly it opens up this show.

Similarly, with *24*, we thought maybe we'll get through twelve episodes, but what happens after the breakfast, which is eight hours from now? It just happened to be something that kept on going; the engine of the show was surprising to us. Even after that first year, we said, "Well, we did it, but there's no way that we can do it again." The studio said there's no way you can do it again. It was this constant challenge, and the show has changed.

The show has changed, not through any conscious will. It's told from the spine of this character, Jack Bauer (Kiefer Sutherland), and year to year he's had these aspirations. The first year he wanted to get his family back together again; his work had taken him away, he's had this affair, he wanted to repair his marriage, and he wanted to deal with his troubled adolescent daughter. At the end of [season one], he saves the day, but he loses his wife.

In the second year, he's seeking forgiveness from his daughter, but also to forgive himself. Through the action of stopping this nuclear bomb, he gets to do that. When Audrey comes around in year four, it's a second chance at love and hanging up his six-gun and his spurs, putting on a suit and falling in love. Of course, character is destiny, and this guy's not destined for love. All the stuff that happens, happens, so it's always told from this sort of aspirational angle of what Jack Bauer wants in the world.

After season five—after he lost Audrey—the show has become harder and harder to write. The show has gotten exponentially harder to do. I've been here longer than anyone, but I don't think there's anybody who's been here—Evan, or even Joel or Bob—who would say this show hasn't gotten harder and harder to do.

Like I told you with *X-Files*, you've really been over so much of the character, and so much of this character's story's been told, that it's harder to find stories that are relatable. After he's lost his wife and the second love of his life and his daughter's forgiveness, there's not a lot he has left in the world; he's kind of this noirish, existentially bereft character whose dealing with only himself in the world.

Are you saying there are no lighthearted *24* episodes in season seven?
There are no lighthearted episodes in season seven.

It's interesting, because the pace of the whole show has gotten very accelerated. Even in that first year, we allowed it to breathe more. There are whole episodes where Jack doesn't even come in 'til the second act, and what happens is actually very understated and very small. We have just gotten to this place where we've all gotten fairly revved up and cranked up and very Jack-centric in the stories.

Steven Moffat of *Doctor Who* has said that television shows evolve into what the audience believes them to be. Do you think that accounts for *24*'s acceleration?
That's very interesting, and kind of true.

After season one finished, was there any discussion of changing the format of the show for year two?
Yeah, the network actually asked us to experiment. Joel [Surnow] and Mike [Loceff], his writing partner, wrote a story that took place in the course of a single day. I think they did it half-heartedly, and it was really to illustrate more to themselves than to the studio that the premise

really was real time; that's what it is, and that's what the promise of the show is.

Similarly, we promised in the very first year not to have cliffhangers; it was a hollow promise, and one we sort of never had any intention of carrying out. The conventional wisdom of the time was cliffhangers are alienating; no one wants to be left hanging by a cliffhanger. I think the opposite would be true, that's how soap operas go on for years.

Also, no one knew that DVRs and DVDs were going to become so popular.

To what extent do you plot the season at the start of the year?
Zero. I always have said that we're lucky to know where we're going to begin, let alone know where we're going to end.

If the dramatic proposition of—for instance, year two—is Jack has to forgive himself and there's redemption at hand, you understand the emotional underpinnings of a show, you have some idea of how it might conclude. Either it turns out well or it doesn't, but at least you know what you're promising dramatically.

Often, we don't decide [how a season's going to end], which gives it this energy of improvisation. We don't plan it out, and so that accounts for some of the improbable twists that we wind up taking, but it's also what keeps it fresh and interesting.

It also keeps the actors from playing the result.
Yes. Absolutely. If the actors know where they're going, they'll play to it and it'll get all fucked up.

So Gregory Itzen couldn't play President Logan as conniving and evil until he got the script saying that he was conniving and evil?
Exactly. [The actors] have to trust us, that we have actually back-filled it all in a sensible enough fashion.

Are you constantly referring back to earlier episodes to check plot twists for plausibility?
Oh, god, yeah. We go through like archivists. If it's a good enough [narrative] place to go, we will absolutely contort ourselves, and maybe even twist the internal logic of what we've seen to make something good pay off.

An old motto we learned that we all talked about way at the beginning of the show is "not good, never boring."

Can you describe the process of breaking an episode?
It's very much like the scripts, very moment to moment. You're scripting one long story, with cliffhangers and digressions and chapters, but the process is just painstaking. Sometimes, it's what's the premise of the episode? What happens if this happens? Sometimes it's just slogging through the mud and just continuing the story that came before.

The good and the bad news of this is that the show is bound by what came before, and limited by what you know has to come after, so there's only so far you can go. The process is not unlike *X-Files* in that it's difficult to find something interesting in real time. What can happen in this short length of time, in this very limited timeframe that's interesting? That's the biggest challenge.

People don't change very often in the course of a single day, really, and they certainly don't change much hour to hour. The dramatic epiphanies that most shows rely on—the so-called arc of the character—is almost invisible in our show. [The challenge is] endowing these real-time moments with significance.

In season six, the nuclear threat is done seven hours before the season ends. Was that to make the narrative less predictable?
It wasn't as conscious as that. It was what had to happen, based on the premise that we came up with.

[After season five concluded with Jack in Chinese custody,] people asked, Is Jack going to be in China [for season six]? No one seemed to realize that if Jack started in China, it would take him three quarters of the season to get him back to LA. Certain things that had to happen to accommodate the story, the corner we'd painted ourselves into at the end of season five.

Jack had to be traded [back to the US] while the shit had already hit the fan. It did create a catch-up mode that was really out of synch and atypical for what we usually do on *24*, which I thought was successful. I was pretty happy with it in the end. It was a story that embraced Jack's sacrifice, and summed up all we had seen to that moment.

How did the WGA strike affect your plans for season seven?[51]

It delayed them, and in a crazy way, the show benefitted from it. We had a couple of rocky false starts, and we pushed production a couple of times.[52] Finding the right story for season seven took two false starts, so we really got off in a wrong footed way.

We completed eight episodes before the strike hit, and it was probably a good time to take a breather and take stock of where we were.

When we came back, the network ordered this prequel, which has come out pretty good. I didn't want to do it when they asked for it, and I resisted as long as I could. They forced my hand, and in the end, I'm glad they did because I think it's going to help ground what we've got emotionally. It's a very good run up to the season proper.[53]

Who wrote the prequel?

I did.

Is there anything you can say about the story?

---

[51] From season four onward, *24* was broadcast without preemption from January to May each year. The WGA strike, which ran from November 2007 to February 2008, interrupted the production of season seven to such an extent that Fox decided to delay the season from 2008 to 2009, creating a twenty-month gap between Day 6 and Day 7.

[52] "Pushing production" means standing down the crew while scripts are finalized before going to the set. It is a costly endeavor that most productions try to avoid.

[53] *24: Redemption*, a two-hour movie broadcast by Fox on 23 November 2008, was produced to be broadcast between Day 6 and Day 7 of the series proper, and established several plot points for season seven, which began in January 2009.

It takes place in Africa, for one thing. Looking at the show strictly from Jack's emotional perspective, he's on the cliff at the end of last year. It's a very "To be, or not to be" moment, and this year, he starts out on trial, answering to congress about his behavior, about his conduct—torture, illegal detentions, all the things that the show itself kinda got brought to task for by the media. Abu Graib and Guantanamo suddenly became things that we were responsible for. The show was in this unfortunate position of having to answer for current events, in a way.

Between that cliff moment and the start of this year, there was a bridge that was missing emotionally. How did Jack get from there to here; the prequel answers that.

Does the prequel take place across two hours?
It does. It's in real-time.

We have been—up 'til now—very good about understanding the transition of power from president to president. We know the relationship of one president to the next and how that happened. In [season seven], we jumped it, and presupposed this female president (Cherry Jones) who we'd never seen before. In the prequel, we dramatized this transfer of power.

What do you look for in hiring writers for *24*?
As it turns out, I look for age and experience.

You seem to have a lot of former showrunners on staff.
Yeah. The show has a very high degree of difficulty. I know everybody

always says that about their show, but this does. Having been around, I've known enough people who've impressed me, so that I do tend to hire people I know and people I know can do the job. A lot of people here now are people I've worked with before.

How has it been to have Alex Gansa join the staff fifteen years after you went your separate ways?
It's been terrific. I've worked with everyone here—David Fury, Manny Coto, Alex—on various shows over the years, and it's a real treat to hire people whom you admire so much.

What advice would you give a writer just starting out in tv?
Keep writing. Be persistent. Be good. Be hard on yourself. That's the best advice I'd give anybody.

People who are too pleased with their work, more often than not, are not looking at themselves hard enough.

What does television have over movies?
Television has a more penetrating influence on the culture. People live longer with the characters. You know Tony Soprano a lot more than you do any of the characters in *The Godfather*.

WHERE ARE THEY NOW?

After co-writing, producing, and directing *The X-Files: I Want to Believe*, CHRIS CARTER created *The After* (2014) for Amazon, but the pilot—which he wrote and directed—did not progress to series. In 2015, Carter reunited with Glen Morgan, James Wong, and Darin Morgan to produce a six-episode revival of *The X-Files* for Fox. Carter wrote and directed three of the episodes.

FRANK SPOTNITZ relocated to Paris after *The X-Files: I Want to Believe*. He's worked on *Strike Back* (2011) for Sky and Cinemax and *The Transporter* (2014) for international broadcast. In 2012, Spotnitz created *Hunted* (2012) for Cinemax and the BBC. Most recently, he adapted Philip K. Dick's Hugo Award-winning novel THE MAN IN THE HIGH CASTLE for Amazon. The series has been renewed for a second season.

Breaking Bad (2008–13) won the Primetime Emmy Award for Outstanding Drama Series in 2013 and 2014. VINCE GILLIGAN— personally Emmy nominated three times for Outstanding Directing for a Drama Series and once for Outstanding Writing for a Drama Series—has become one of the most-recognized showrunners of what has been hailed as a new golden age of television. In February 2016, he and co-creator Peter Gould will launch the second season of the *Breaking Bad* spinoff, *Better Call Saul* (2015–), which was nominated for seven Primetime Emmys—including Outstanding Drama Series—in its freshman season.

JOHN SHIBAN followed up his three year stint as consulting producer (and occasional director) on *Breaking Bad* (2009–11), with two scripts for *Torchwood: Miracle Day* (2011). He served as executive producer for AMC's *Hell on Wheels* (2011–2), and most recently for Starz's *Da Vinci's Demons* (2015), which he shepherded to its conclusion.

After *24* concluded its original run in 2010, HOWARD GORDON and Alex Gansa developed *Homeland* (2011–) for Showtime, from a script by Gideon Raff. Not content to have one series on the schedule, Gordon has produced *Awake* (2012) for NBC, *24: Live Another Day* (2014) for Fox, *Tyrant* (2014–) for FX, *Legends* (2014–) for TNT, and *Second Chance* (2016–) for Fox. With Gansa and Raff, he won the 2012 Primetime Emmy Award for Outstanding Writing for a Drama Series for the pilot of *Homeland*.

Appendix: WRITING CREDITS

Episodes noted with an asterisk were also directed by the writer.

CHRIS CARTER
Season One (1993–4) Creator/Executive Producer
1X79 Pilot
1X01 Deep Throat
1X04 The Jersey Devil
1X08 Space
1X11 Fire
1X15 Young at Heart (with Scott Kaufer)
1X19 Darkness Falls
1X23 The Erlenmeyer Flask

Season Two (1994–5) Creator/Executive Producer
2X02 The Host
2X05 Duane Barry*
2X10 Red Museum
2X13 Irresistible
2X16 Colony (story by Duchovny & Carter)
2X22 F. Emasculata (with Gordon)
2X25 Anasazi (story by Duchovny & Carter)

Season Three (1995–6) Creator/Executive Producer
3X01 The Blessing Way
3X02 Paper Clip
3X05 The List*
3X09 Nisei (with Gordon & Spotnitz)
3X13 Syzygy

3X15 Piper Maru (with Spotnitz)

3X16 Apocrypha (with Spotnitz)

3X24 Talitha Cumi (story by Duchovny & Carter)

Season Four (1996–7) Creator/Executive Producer

4X01 Herrenvolk

4X09 Tunguska (with Spotnitz)

4X10 Terma (with Spotnitz)

4X15 Momento Mori (with Gilligan & Shiban & Spotnitz)

4X16 Unrequited (with Gordon, from Gordon's story)

4X17 Tempus Fugit (with Spotnitz)

4X18 Max (with Spotnitz)

4X24 Gethsemane

Theatrical Film (1997–8) Producer

The X-Files: Fight the Future (story by Carter & Spotnitz)

NOTE: Though written and produced between seasons four and five, the feature film was released the summer of 1998, between years five and six of the series.

Season Five (1997–8) Creator/Executive Producer

5X02 Redux

5X03 Redux II

5X06 The Post-Modern Prometheus*

5X10 Chinga (with Stephen King)

5X13 Patient X (with Spotnitz)

5X14 The Red and the Black (with Spotnitz)

5X20 The End

Season Six (1998–9) Creator/Executive Producer

6ABX01 The Beginning

6ABX03 Triangle*

6ABX08 How the Ghosts Stole Christmas

6ABX11 Two Fathers (with Spotnitz)

6ABX12 One Son (with Spotnitz)

6ABX18 Milagro (story by Shiban & Spotnitz)

6ABX22 Biogenesis (with Spotnitz)

Season Seven (1999-2000) Creator/Executive Producer

7ABX03 The Sixth Extinction

7ABX04 The Sixth Extinction II: Amor Fati (with Duchovny)

7ABX10 Sein und Zeit (with Spotnitz)

7ABX11 Closure (with Spotnitz)

7ABX13 First Person Shooter (by William Gibson & Tom Maddox)*

7ABX20 Fight Club

7ABX22 Requiem

Season Eight (2000–1) Creator/Executive Producer

8ABX01 Within

8ABX02 Without

8ABX04 Patience*

8ABX08 Per Manum (with Spotnitz)

8ABX14 This Is Not Happening (with Spotnitz)

8ABX15 DeadAlive (with Spotnitz)

8ABX18 Three Words (with Spotnitz)

8ABX20 Essence

8ABX21 Existence

Season Nine (2001–2) Creator/Executive Producer

9ABX01 Nothing Important Happened Today (with Spotnitz)

9ABX02 Nothing Important Happened Today II (with Spotnitz)

9ABX08 Trust No 1 (with Spotnitz)

9ABX10 Provenance (with Spotnitz)

9ABX11 Providence (with Spotnitz)*

9ABX14 Improbable*
9ABX17 William (story by Duchovny & Spotnitz & Carter)
9ABX19/9ABX20 The Truth

Theatrical Film (2007–8) Producer
The X-Files: I Want to Believe (with Spotnitz)*

Season Ten (2016) Creator/Executive Producer
1AYW01 My Struggle*
1AYW04 Babylon*
1AYW06 My Struggle II*

FRANK SPOTNITZ

Season Two (1995) Staff Writer

2X19 End Game

2X24 Our Town

Season Three (1995–6) Story Editor

3X09 Nisei (with Carter & Gordon)

3X10 731

3X15 Piper Maru (with Carter)

3X16 Apocrypha (with Carter)

Season Four (1996–7) Co-Producer

4X09 Tunguska (with Carter)

4X10 Terma (with Carter)

4X14 Leonard Betts (with Gilligan & Shiban)

4X15 Momento Mori (with Carter & Gilligan & Shiban)

4X17 Tempus Fugit (with Carter)

4X18 Max (with Carter)

4X21 Zero Sum (with Gordon)

Theatrical Film (1997–8)

The X-Files: Fight the Future (by Carter, story by Carter & Spotnitz)

NOTE: Though written and produced between seasons four and five, the feature film was released the summer of 1998, between years five and six of the series.

Season Five (1997–8) Co-Executive Producer

5X04 Detour

5X05 A Christmas Carol (with Gilligan & Shiban)

5X07 Emily (with Gilligan & Shiban)

5X13 Patient X (with Carter)

5X14 The Red and the Black (with Carter)

5X15 Travelers (with Shiban)

5X17 All Souls (with Shiban, story by Billy Brown & Dan Angel)

Season Six (1998–9) Executive Producer

6ABX04 Dreamland (with Gilligan & Shiban)

6ABX05 Dreamland II (with Gilligan & Shiban)

6ABX11 Two Fathers (with Carter)

6ABX12 One Son (with Carter)

6ABX18 Milagro (by Carter, story by Shiban & Spotnitz)

6ABX21 Field Trip (by Gilligan & Shiban, story by Spotnitz)

6ABX22 Biogenesis (with Carter)

Season Seven (1999-2000) Executive Producer

7ABX05 Millennium (with Gilligan)

7ABX08 The Amazing Maleeni (with Gilligan & Shiban)

7ABX10 Sein und Zeit (with Carter)

7ABX11 Closure (with Carter)

7ABX14 Theef (with Gilligan & Shiban)

Season Eight (2000–1) Executive Producer

8ABX07 Via Negativa

8ABX08 Per Manum (with Carter)

8ABX11 The Gift

8ABX13 Medusa

8ABX14 This Is Not Happening (with Carter)

8ABX15 DeadAlive (with Carter)

8ABX18 Three Words (with Carter)

8ABX19 Alone*

Season Nine (2001–2) Executive Producer

9ABX01 Nothing Important Happened Today (with Carter)

9ABX02 Nothing Important Happened Today II (with Carter)

9ABX03 Dæmonicus*

9ABX08 Trust No 1 (with Carter)
9ABX10 Provenance (with Carter)
9ABX11 Providence (with Carter)
9ABX15 Jump the Shark (with Gilligan & Shiban)
9ABX17 William (by Carter, story by Duchovny & Spotnitz & Carter)

Theatrical Film (2007–8) Producer

The X-Files: I Want to Believe (with Carter)

VINCE GILLIGAN
Season Two (1995) Freelance Writer
2X23 Soft Light
Season Three (1995–6) Creative Consultant
3X17 Pusher
Season Four (1996–7) Co-Producer
4X02 Unruhe
4X08 Paper Hearts
4X14 Leonard Betts (with Shiban & Spotnitz)
4X15 Momento Mori (with Carter & Shiban & Spotnitz)
4X20 Small Potatoes
Season Five (1997–8) Supervising Producer
5X01 Unusual Suspects
5X05 A Christmas Carol (with Shiban & Spotnitz)
5X07 Emily (with Shiban & Spotnitz)
5X08 Kitsunegari (with Tim Minear)
5X12 Bad Blood
5X19 Folie à Deux
Season Six (1998–9) Co-Executive Producer
6ABX02 Drive
6ABX04 Dreamland (with Shiban & Spotnitz)
6ABX05 Dreamland II (with Shiban & Spotnitz)
6ABX09 Tithonus
6ABX15 Monday (with Shiban)
6ABX19 Three of a Kind (with Shiban)
6ABX21 Field Trip (by Gilligan & Shiban, story by Spotnitz)
Season Seven (1999-2000) Co-Executive Producer
7ABX01 Monster

7ABX05 Millennium (with Spotnitz)
7ABX08 The Amazing Maleeni (with Shiban & Spotnitz)
7ABX12 X-Cops
7ABX14 Theef (with Shiban & Spotnitz)
7ABX21 Je Souhaite*

Season Eight (2000–1) Executive Producer
8ABX05 Roadrunners

Season Nine (2001–2) Executive Producer
9ABX07 John Doe
9ABX15 Jump the Shark (with Shiban & Spotnitz)
9ABX18 Sunshine Days*

JOHN SHIBAN
Season Three (1995–6) Staff Writer
3X07 The Walk
3X18 Teso dos Bichos
Season Four (1996–7) Story Editor
4X11 El Mundo Gira
4X14 Leonard Betts (with Gilligan & Spotnitz)
4X15 Momento Mori (with Carter & Gilligan & Spotnitz)
4X22 Elegy
Season Five (1997–8) Co-Producer
5X05 A Christmas Carol (with Gilligan & Spotnitz)
5X07 Emily (with Gilligan & Spotnitz)
5X15 Travelers (with Spotnitz)
5X17 All Souls (with Spotnitz, story by Billy Brown & Dan Angel)
5X18 The Pine Bluff Variant
Season Six (1998–9) Producer
6ABX04 Dreamland (with Gilligan & Spotnitz)
6ABX05 Dreamland II (with Gilligan & Spotnitz)
6ABX10 S.R. 819
6ABX15 Monday (with Gilligan)
6ABX18 Milagro (by Carter, story by Shiban & Spotnitz)
6ABX19 Three of a Kind (with Gilligan)
6ABX21 Field Trip (by Gilligan & Shiban, story by Spotnitz)
Season Seven (1999-2000) Supervising Producer
7ABX08 The Amazing Maleeni (with Gilligan & Spotnitz)
7ABX14 Theef (with Gilligan & Spotnitz)
Season Eight (2000–1) Co-Executive Producer
8ABX12 Badlaa

Season Nine (2001–2) Executive Producer

9ABX09 Underneath*

9ABX15 Jump the Shark (with Gilligan & Spotnitz)

9ABX16 Release (teleplay by Amann, story by Amann & Shiban)

HOWARD GORDON

Season One (1993–4) Supervising Producer

1X03 Conduit (with Gansa)

1X06 Ghost in the Machine (with Gansa)

1X09 Fallen Angel (with Gansa)

1X14 Lazarus (with Gansa)

1X17 Miracle Man (with Carter)

1X21 Born Again (with Gansa)

Season Two (1994–5) Supervising Producer

2X04 Sleepless

2X09 Firewalker

2X15 Fresh Bones

2X19 Død Kalm (story by Gordon & Gansa)

2x22 F. Emasculata (with Carter)

Season Three (1995–6) Co-Executive Producer

3X03 D.P.O.

3X09 Nisei (with Carter & Spotnitz)

3X14 Grotesque

3X21 Avatar (story by Duchovny & Gordon)

Season Four (1996–7) Executive Producer

4X04 Teliko

4X12 Kaddish

4X16 Unrequited (with Carter, from Gordon's story)

4X19 Synchrony (with David Greenwalt)

4X21 Zero Sum (with Spotnitz)

This book would not have been possible
without the support of my wife
CYNTHIA DAVIS
who was suitably impressed that I'd interned
at Ten Thirteen when she met me five years later.

JASON DAVIS is an award-winning writer who's contributed hundreds of articles to various print and online publications, published several short stories, and created and produced the television series STUDIO THIRTEEN for SATURDAY NIGHT LIVE creator Lorne Michaels. He's edited fifteen books by the legendary Harlan Ellison® and over a dozen books on the television series BABYLON 5. He lives in Burbank with his wife.

He can be found on the internet at:
HumanityIsMyBusiness.com
and
HarlanEllisonBooks.com

Or on Twitter:
@thejasondavis

Made in United States
Troutdale, OR
03/13/2024